SHEPHERD'S NOTES

Shepherd's Notes Titles Available

SHEPHERD'S NOTES COMMENTARY SERIES

Old Testament

0-80549-028-0	Genesis	0-80549-341-7	Psalms 101-150
0-80549-056-6	Exodus	0-80549-016-7	Proverbs
0-80549-069-8	Leviticus & Numbers	0-80549-059-0	Ecclesiastes, Song of Solomon
0-80549-027-2	Deuteronomy		
0-80549-058-2	Joshua & Judges	0-80549-197-X	Isaiah
0-80549-057-4	Ruth & Esther	0-80549-070-1	Jeremiah-Lamentations
0-80549-063-9	1 & 2 Samuel		
0-80549-007-8	1 & 2 Kings	0-80549-078-7	Ezekiel
0-80549-064-7	1 & 2 Chronicles	0-80549-015-9	Daniel
0-80549-194-5	Ezra, Nehemiah	0-80549-326-3	Hosea-Obadiah
0-80549-006-X	Job	0-80549-334-4	Jonah-Zephaniah
0-80549-339-5	Psalms 1-50	0-80549-065-5	Haggai-Malachi
0-80549-340-9	Psalms 51-100		

New Testament

1-55819-688-9	Matthew	1-55819-689-7	Philippians, Colossians, & Philemon
0-80549-071-X	Mark		
0-80549-004-3	Luke		
1-55819-693-5	John	0-80549-000-0	1 & 2 Thessalonians
1-55819-691-9	Acts	1-55819-692-7	1 & 2 Timothy, Titus
0-80549-005-1	Romans	0-80549-336-0	Hebrews
0-80549-325-5	1 Corinthians	0-80549-018-3	James
0-80549-335-2	2 Corinthians	0-80549-019-1	1 & 2 Peter & Jude
1-55819-690-0	Galatians	0-80549-214-3	1, 2 & 3 John
0-80549-327-1	Ephesians	0-80549-017-5	Revelation

SHEPHERD'S NOTES CHRISTIAN CLASSICS

0-80549-347-6	Mere Christianity-C.S.Lewis	0-80549-394-8	Miracles-C.S.Lewis
0-80549-353-0	The Problem of Pain/ A Grief Observed-C.S.Lewis	0-80549-196-1	Lectures to My Students-Charles Haddon Spurgeon
0-80549-199-6	The Confessions-Augustine	0-80549-220-8	The Writings of Justin Martyr
0-80549-200-3	Calvin's Institutes	0-80549-345-X	The City of God

SHEPHERD'S NOTES-BIBLE SUMMARY SERIES

0-80549-377-8	Old Testament	0-80549-385-9	Life & Letters of Paul
0-80549-378-6	New Testament	0-80549-376-X	Manners & Customs of Bible Times
0-80549-384-0	Life & Teachings of Jesus	0-80549-380-8	Basic Christian Beliefs

SHEPHERD'S NOTES

When you need a guide through the Scriptures

II Corinthians

HOLMAN
REFERENCE

Nashville, Tennessee

Shepherds Notes—*2 Corinthians*
© 1998 Broadman & Holman Publishers, Nashville, Tennessee
All rights reserved
Printed in the United States of America

ISBN# 0-8054-9335-2

Dewey Decimal Classification: 227.307
Subject Heading: BIBLE. N.T. CORINTHIANS
Library of Congress Card Catalog Number: 98-23137

Library of Congress Cataloging-in-Publication Data

Gould, Dana, 1951–

    2 Corinthians / Dana Gould, editor [i.e. author].

      p. cm. — (Shepherd's notes)

    Includes bibliographical references.

    ISBN 0-8054-9335-2 (pbk.)

    1. Bible. N.T. Corinthians —Study and teaching.   I. Title.

II. Series

BS2675.5.G68   1998

227'.307—dc21   98-27137
                                              CIP

2 3 4 5 6 7 08 07 06 05

CONTENTS

Dear Reader:

Shepherd's Notes are designed to give you a quick, step-by-step overview of every book of the Bible. They are not meant to be substitutes for the biblical text; rather, they are study guides intended to help you explore the wisdom of Scripture in personal or group study and to apply that wisdom successfully in your own life.

Shepherd's Notes guide you through the main themes of each book of the Bible and illuminate fascinating details through appropriate commentary and reference notes. Historical and cultural background information bring the Bible into sharper focus.

Six different icons, used throughout the series, call your attention to historical-cultural information, Old Testament and New Testament references, word pictures, unit summaries, and personal application for everyday life.

Whether you are a novice or a veteran at Bible study, I believe you will find *Shepherd's Notes* a resource that will take you to a new level in your mining and applying the riches of Scripture.

In Him,

David R. Shepherd
Editor-in-Chief

How to Use This Book

DESIGNED FOR THE BUSY USER

Shepherd's Notes for 2 Corinthians is designed to provide an easy-to-use tool for getting a quick handle on this Bible book's important features, and for gaining an understanding of the message of 2 Corinthians. Information available in more difficult-to-use reference works has been incorporated into the *Shepherd's Notes* format. This brings you the benefits of many more advanced and expensive works packed into one small volume.

Shepherd's Notes are for laymen, pastors, teachers, small-group leaders and participants, as well as the classroom student. Enrich your personal study or quiet time. Shorten your class or small-group preparation time as you gain valuable insights into the truths of God's Word that you can pass along to your students or group members.

DESIGNED FOR QUICK ACCESS

Those with time constraints will especially appreciate the timesaving features built in the *Shepherd's Notes*. All features are intended to aid a quick and concise encounter with the heart of the message.

Concise Commentary. Short sections provide quick "snapshots" of passages, highlighting important points and other information.

Outlined Text. A comprehensive outline covers the entire text of 2 Corinthians. This is a valuable feature for following the narrative's flow, allowing for a quick, easy way to locate a particular passage.

Shepherd's Notes. These summary statements appear at the close of every key section of the narrative. While functioning in part as a quick summary, they also deliver the essence of the message presented in the sections they cover.

Icons. Various icons in the margin highlight recurring themes in 2 Corinthians, aiding in selective searching or tracing of those themes.

Sidebars and Charts. These specially selected features provide additional background information to your study or preparation. These include definitions as well as cultural, historical, and biblical insights.

Maps. These are placed at appropriate places in the book to aid your understanding and study of a text or passage.

Questions to Guide Your Study. These thought-provoking questions and discussion starters are designed to encourage interaction with the truth and principles of God's Word.

In addition to the above features, study aids have been included at the back of the book for those readers who require or desire more information and resources for working through 2 Corinthians. These include chapter outlines for studying 2 Corinthians and a list of reference sources used for this volume, which offer many works that allow the reader to extend the scope of his or her study of this letter.

DESIGNED TO WORK FOR YOU

Personal Study. Using the *Shepherd's Notes* with a passage of Scripture can enlighten your study and take it to a new level. At your fingertips is information that would require searching several volumes to find. In addition, many points of application occur throughout the volume, contributing to personal growth.

Teaching. Outlines frame the text of 2 Corinthians and provide a logical presentation of the message. Shepherd's Notes provide summary statements for presenting the essence of key points and events. Personal Application icons point out personal application of the message of 2 Corinthians, and Historical Context icons indicate where background information is supplied.

Group Study. *Shepherd's Notes* can be an excellent companion volume to use for gaining a quick but accurate understanding of the message of a Bible book. Each group member can benefit by having his or her own copy. The *Notes'* format accommodates the study of or the tracing of themes throughout 2 Corinthians. Leaders may use its flexible features to prepare for group sessions, or use them during group sessions. "Questions to Guide Your Study" can spark discussion of the key points and truths of 2 Corinthians.

LIST OF MARGIN ICONS USED IN 2 CORINTHIANS

Shepherd's Notes. Placed at the end of each section, a capsule statement provides the reader with the essence of the message of that section.

Historical Context. To indicate background information—historical, biographical, cultural—and provide insight on the understanding or interpretation of a passage.

Old Testament Reference. To indicate an Old Testament passage that illuminates a passage in 2 Corinthians.

New Testament Reference. Used when the writer refers to New Testament passages that are either fulfilled prophecy, an antitype of an Old Testament type, or a New Testament text which in some other way illuminates the passages under discussion.

Personal Application. Used when the text provides a personal or universal application of truth.

Word Picture. Indicates that the meaning of a specific word or phrase is illustrated so as to shed light on it.

INTRODUCTION

This is Paul's most personal and pastoral letter. While it is a different kind of letter than Romans or even 1 Corinthians, it is characterized by his style. It contains some of Paul's most profound theology. In this letter he reveals more about himself and his feelings than in any of his other writings. Yet, this book is probably less read and understood than any of his other letters. This second letter to the Corinthians is third in length among his New Testament letters, second only to Romans and 1 Corinthians.

SECOND CORINTHIANS IN A "NUTSHELL"

Purpose:	To prepare readers for Paul's third visit and to defend Paul and the gospel he taught against false teachers.
Key Passage:	2 Cor. 5:11, 12
Major Doctrines:	The church, Jesus Christ, and salvation
Letter's Influence:	C. K. Barrett called 2 Corinthians "the fullest and most passionate account of what Paul meant by apostleship."

AUTHOR

The apostle Paul is the author of 2 Corinthians (1:1; 10:1). An internal comparison of both 1 and 2 Corinthians strongly supports this claim. The Pauline authorship of 2 Corinthians is accepted by both the early and the present church.

The Apostle Paul

Paul is the official name of this outstanding missionary apostle (Paul's Jewish name was Saul). He was born on Turkey's southern shore in Tarsus. Well trained in Jewish Scriptures and tradition, he also learned the trade of tentmaking. He was the author of thirteen New Testament epistles.

Paul's third missionary journey centered in Ephesus, from which the gospel probably spread into the surrounding cities. From Ephesus he carried on a correspondence with the Corinthian church. While in Corinth at the end of this journey, he wrote his epistle to the Romans.

Audience

Paul wrote to the church at Corinth—a body of believers who had come out of an exceptionally pagan environment and culture. The church had several problems, among them a leadership problem producing divisions in the church (1 Cor. 1:10–17). Immoral practices were not being dealt with (1 Cor. 5:1–6:20). An enthusiastic group in the church flaunted their spiritual gifts (1 Cor. 12:1–14:40). A legalistic group was concerned about dietary laws (1 Cor. 8:1–10:32). Some were abusing the Lord's Supper (1 Cor. 11:17–34), and others were offering false teachings regarding the Resurrection (1 Cor. 15:1–58). These matters—in addition to its multiethnic makeup of Greeks, Romans, and Jews and a mixture of social classes including rich, poor, and slave—made for a unique and troubled congregation.

PURPOSE FOR WRITING

Paul's primary purpose for writing 2 Corinthians was to prepare the Corinthian believers for his coming visit. Paul wrote this letter at a time when relations between him and the church at Corinth were strained. In this letter, Paul expressed relief that the crisis at Corinth showed signs of subsiding.

DATE OF WRITING

This letter is difficult to date, for we do not know the amount of time that separated 1 and 2 Corinthians. The content of the letter suggests that Paul wrote it soon after writing 1 Corinthians. The letter has been variously dated between A.D. 55 and 57.

THE UNITY OF THE LETTER

Some have suggested that chapters 10–13 were the severe (or painful) letter, written prior to chapters 1–9; but strong evidence for this is lacking. Most likely the severe letter has not survived. The letter, as we now have it, forms a coherent whole as the structure and outline indicate. The history of the church has been nearly unanimous in affirming the letter's unity. No existing Greek manuscripts present the letter in any other form.

THE DOCTRINES OF 2 CORINTHIANS

Dominant themes include Paul's gratitude to God and Christ (1:3; 5:14) and his ministry as a continuing triumph in Christ (2:14). Paul shared the risen life of Christ (4:10–11). Simultaneously he gloried in infirmities and was content with weaknesses, persecutions, and calamities for the sake of Christ (12:9). His ministry was characterized by integrity and suffering (1:8–12; 6:3–10; 11:23–29), marks of a true apostle. His message as an ambassador of Christ focused on the message of reconciliation (5:11–21) and Jesus Christ as Lord (4:5).

Paul's collection for the church at Jerusalem had an important role in his missionary efforts. He devoted two chapters to this matter (chaps. 8–9). They provide some of the most helpful teaching on Christian stewardship found in the New Testament.

THE THEOLOGICAL SIGNIFICANCE OF 2 CORINTHIANS

In this letter we learn of the importance of restoring relationships in ministry. An important lesson on dealing with opponents and appealing to God for confirmation of one's ministry is contained herein. The most important aspect of this letter is Paul's inspired insights regarding the nature of ministry. Ministry involves suffering, joy, comfort, and hard work. Primarily, ministry is the power of God working in and through His people to accomplish His purposes.

We learn of the importance of sacrificial and spontaneous giving. These important principles regarding Christian stewardship need to be expounded in every congregation. Believers are to follow Christ in giving freely with joy and love.

Finally, we learn of the significance of Christ's reconciling work in restoring our broken relationship with God. Because of what He has done for us, we are a new creation, participants in the new covenant, and His ambassadors to proclaim the message of reconciliation. Because believers have been reconciled to God, they should be reconciled to other believers.

The City of Corinth

The city of Corinth was located on a narrow strip of land that connected the Peloponnesian Peninsula with northern Greece. It had two seaports, Cenchrea on the Aegean side in the east and Lechaeum at the edge of the gulf of Corinth in the west. The city's location made it a crossroads for travel and commerce and contributed to its prosperity. Ship captains, eager to avoid the stormy dangers of sailing around the Peloponnesian Straits on the south, would dock at one port of Corinth. Their cargo was unloaded, hauled overland, and then loaded in another vessel on the opposite side. They avoided the risk of losing ships and lives in the dangerous voyage along the southern route.

Corinth was also known for hosting athletic events known as the Isthmian games. These events took place every two years and provided great financial rewards to the victors. Huge crowds thronged to the city for the festivities.

THE RELEVANCE OF 2 CORINTHIANS FOR CHRISTIANS TODAY

Second Corinthians was written from the heart of a great church leader. Because it was addressed to specific situations in the life of the church, it speaks as directly to the church today as it did to its original readers. Several relevant topics surface in Paul's second letter to the Corinthians, as shown below.

Suffering. Everyone experiences pain and distress in life. Suffering is one of Paul's major themes in 2 Corinthians. His inspired understanding of suffering speaks to every Christian. God gives the comfort and strength necessary to turn misery into ministry. As we see in Paul's life, suffering equips the Christian for ministry.

Ministry. "What is the ministry of the church?" is a question raised by each generation of believers. Paul's answer is that the church is a ministry of reconciliation that urges persons to be reconciled to God. Such a ministry requires that the church model Jesus Christ.

Leadership and authority. Paul offers the pattern of Christlike leadership. This kind of leadership is centered in the example of Christ. The authority to lead comes only by sharing in the suffering of Christ.

The nature of the gospel. Human nature resists the implications of the gospel. There is a strong tendency to substitute schemes of human effort. Believers are newly created in Christ and have a new nature. This new nature is to determine the way believers live in the world.

Christian giving. Today's culture, as was Paul's, is characterized by luxury, materialism, and inequality. Paul placed a strong emphasis on giving. Christian stewardship is based on the fact that God is a generous giver. He can continue to supply our needs as we give to others.

A CHRONOLOGY OF PAUL'S RELATIONSHIP WITH THE CORINTHIAN CHURCH

1. Paul evangelized Corinth during his second journey (Acts 18:1–11).
2. Paul wrote a letter to Corinth, now lost, in which he urged Christians to avoid association with professing believers who were immoral (1 Cor. 5:9–11).
3. Paul wrote 1 Corinthians from Ephesus during his third missionary journey to advise the Corinthians on handling problems in the church.
4. Paul made a "painful" visit to Corinth from Ephesus to correct problems in the church. His visit failed to achieve its aim (2 Cor. 2:1).
5. Paul sent another letter, also lost, calling the Corinthians to repentance and urging discipline for an opponent in the church (2 Cor. 2:4–11). Titus carried the letter to Corinth. Scholars have named this letter the "severe" letter.
6. Paul left Ephesus, for Troas and then to Macedonia, to await word on the success of Titus's visit (2 Cor. 2:12, 13).
7. Titus met Paul in Macedonia with the report of the Corinthian church's warm acceptance of Paul's letter and eagerness to see him (2 Cor. 7:5–16).
8. Paul wrote 2 Corinthians from Macedonia and sent it to Corinth by Titus.
9. Paul went to Corinth for his third visit (2 Cor. 12:14; 13:1; Acts 20:2).

(List taken from Thomas D. Lea, *The New Testament: Its Background and Message*, p. 412.)

BASIC OUTLINE FOR 2 CORINTHIANS

I. Introduction (1:1–2)
II. Apostolic Experience (1:3–11)
III. Apostolic Explanation (1:12–2:11)
IV. Apostolic Ministry (2:12–7:16)
V. Apostolic Fellowship (8:1–9:15)
VI. Apostolic Defense (10:1–13:14)

QUESTIONS TO GUIDE YOUR STUDY

1. Who were Paul's readers? Why did he write a follow-up letter to 1 Corinthians?
2. What problems did Paul address at Corinth in this letter?
3. What key doctrines does Paul address in this letter?
4. What is unique about 2 Corinthians?
5. What makes Paul's message in this letter relevant to today's readers?

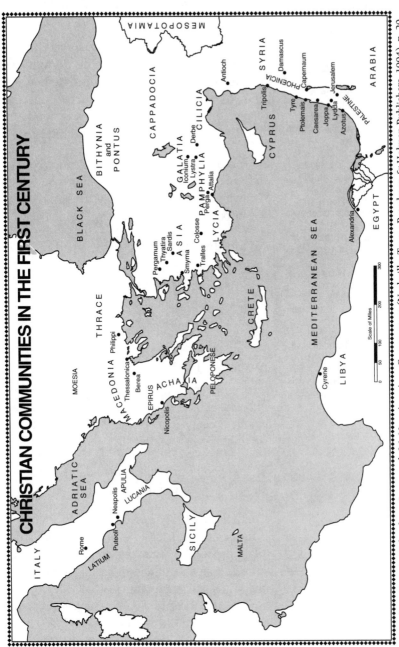

CHRISTIAN COMMUNITIES IN THE FIRST CENTURY

Taken from Kurt A. Richardson, *James*, vol. 36, New American Commentary (Nashville, Tenn.: Broadman & Holman Publishers, 1994), p. 20

The Hellenistic Letter

Generally, Paul's epistles do seem to follow the normal pattern of the hellenistic letter, the basic form of which consists of five major sections:

1. Opening (sender, addressee, greeting);
2. Thanksgiving or blessing (often with prayer of intercession, well wishes, or personal greetings);
3. The Burden of the letter (including citation of classical sources and arguments);
4. Parenesis (ethical instruction, exhortation); and
5. Closing (mention of personal plans, mutual friends, benediction).

In this first chapter Paul defended himself against his former detractors at Corinth and answered some of the attacks directed against him. Identifying himself as an apostle, one specially commissioned by Christ, was significant for Paul's defense of his calling and ministry.

In this opening chapter, Paul introduced one of his major themes in this letter—suffering. Drawing from his own experience, Paul described the value of suffering for the believer.

GREETING (1:1, 2)

Paul followed the pattern of the hellenistic letter, a standard letter form in the ancient world. In his greeting, Paul identified himself as the writer, named his readers, and then gave them a blessing.

Writer (v. 1)

Paul is the author of this letter (1:1: 10:1). It is the apostle's most personal and pastoral letter, and it contains more biographical material than any of his other writings.

In his opening greeting, Paul told us some about himself and his calling.

Paul, an apostle. The designation *apostle* refers to a messenger or delegate—one sent for a particular purpose. It means "one commissioned." An apostle is a person "holding the highest office in the Christian communities" (F. Wilbur Gingrich, *Shorter Lexicon of the Greek New Testament* [Chicago: U. of Chicago Press, 1957], 25). Paul is an apostle of "Christ Jesus by the will of God." Here he emphasized the authority of his commission, which paralleled that of the twelve original apostles.

Timothy, our brother. While on his second missionary journey, Paul met Timothy. Paul recruited him as a member of his missionary team. Timothy is now with Paul, having been sent on to Macedonia from Ephesus (Acts 19:22).

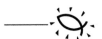

In Matt. 10:40, Jesus commissioned the Twelve. He told them, "He who receives you receives me, and he who receives me receives the one who sent me."

Recipients (v. 1)
To the church of God in Corinth. The audience is the very same church to which he addressed 1 Corinthians: "To the church of God in Corinth" (v. 2). In the ancient world, Corinth was an important city of trade, but it had a reputation for wickedness. The church at Corinth was Gentile, and its converts came from a wide variety of backgrounds and religious experiences. These members had little preparation for living the Christian life, unlike other churches that were made up of God-fearers, proselytes, and Jewish converts. In addressing the believers at Corinth, Paul had to deal with basic moral, church, and doctrinal matters.

With all the saints. "Saints" means "holy ones." They are holy people set apart as God's possession. This is the title given to all believers because they are dedicated to God.

Extended Greeting (v. 2)
Paul's opening greeting to the Corinthians is "grace and peace to you."

Grace. This is God's unmerited favor. In spite of our sin, God loves us. In spite of our unrighteousness, God clothes us with His righteousness. No person can earn this grace; it may only be received through faith.

Peace. This word was a common Jewish greeting. In the New Testament, however, it carries a deeper meaning. To the Jew, this word signified freedom from internal and external conflict. To the Christian, it describes all the blessings of salvation.

"These words, common in Paul's Epistles, bear 'the stamp of Paul's experience' . . . no one word carries more meaning for Paul's messages than this word" (A. T. Robertson, *Word Pictures in the New Testament*, "Epistles of Paul," vol. 4, p. 7).

- ■ *Paul's opening greeting followed the helle-*
- ■ *nistic letter format, but with an extension. He*
- ■ *referred to his divine commission as an apos-*
- ■ *tle. His readers were the members of the*
- ■ *church at Corinth. He called them "saints,"*
- ■ *those who have been sanctified and called to*
- ■ *be separated unto God.*

THANKSGIVING TO GOD (1:3)

The section covering verses 3–11 is an outpouring of praise to God that describes both comfort and suffering. Verse 3 focuses on God and reveals several truths about Him.

The Father of Jesus Christ (v. 3). God is like Jesus, but He is more than Jesus. He is Jesus' "Father."

The Father of compassion (v . 3). This signifies that God is a merciful Father whose character is to show compassion.

The God of all comfort (v. 3). God is the encourager. He is the God of all comfort, which means that His comfort meets every need. Those with troubled hearts may find strength in Him.

Comfort

This noun is a compound word made up of the preposition "alongside" and the verb "to call." It indicates a calling to one's side. Depending on its context, it is translated "exhortation," "consolation," "comfort," or "encouragement." "It is the standing beside a person to encourage him when he is undergoing severe testing" (Fritz Rienecker, *Linguistic Key to the Greek New Testament* [Grand Rapids: Zondervan, 1980], 450).

- *This verse is rich in meaning and truth. It*
- *focuses on God and reveals several truths*
- *about Him. He is the Father of Jesus Christ,*
- *the Father of compassion, and the God of all*
- *comfort (v. 3).*

For those who suffer, God provides strength, and this strength becomes a rich resource for ministering to others. From this passage we see that Paul viewed his suffering as *ministry*, not misery. He provided three purposes of the suffering of God's people.

THE MINISTRY OF SUFFERING (1:4–11)

The Jews expected the time of the Messiah would be preceded by the suffering of His people. It was Jesus, however, who suffered for His people. Those whom He called to follow Him also suffered. Those who choose to engage in Christian service will experience many difficulties, but, Paul teaches that this suffering is not purposeless.

Our sufferings are related to Christ's sufferings. Much of the comfort Paul received during his suffering came from knowing that his suffering was related to "the sufferings of Christ" (v. 5).

Suffering is a part of ministry. Paul used his own suffering as an example for the Corinthians and to witness to God's deliverance. Something terrible had happened to him in Asia (the Roman province around Ephesus). Paul provided no details about the problem, but the best theory is that Paul referred to some serious threat. It might have been the attack on his ministry in Ephesus.

Suffering provides opportunity for partnership in prayer. Although the Corinthians were not mature believers, Paul confessed that he needed their help. The prayers of the Corinthians had helped Paul, and God's blessings had yielded joy and gratitude in their lives. In this way, intercessory prayer is an investment

Through his own experience, Paul taught that through prayer even the weakest believer can help the greatest Christian.

that pays dividends for those who pray as well as for those prayed for. The more prayer is offered, the more thanksgiving there will be when the prayer is answered.

- *Jesus suffered for His people, and those*
- *whom He calls to follow Him will also suffer.*
- *But, Paul taught that there is purpose to the*
- *Christian's suffering. For those who suffer,*
- *God provides strength, and this strength*
- *becomes a rich resource for ministering to*
- *others.*

SOMETHING TO BE PROUD OF (1:12–14)

Verse 12 looks back to verse 11. Paul had a right to ask for the prayers of the Corinthians because his conscience was clear about his behavior toward them. He spoke of a "boast." This word and its related forms occur twenty-nine times in 2 Corinthians, more than in the rest of the New Testament. It is a theme that runs throughout the letter.

Boast

The word *boast* occurs twice in this passage (vv. 12 and 14). Its basic meaning is "that in which one glories, a matter or ground of glorying." The ending of the noun in the original language Paul used to write his letter (Greek), means "the act of glorying" in verse 12, but in verse 14 the word means "the thing boasted of" (Fritz Rienecker, *Linguistic Key to the Greek New Testament* [Grand Rapids: Zondervan, 1980], 452).

Because others were boasting, Paul felt that he must engage in this foolish approach to set the record straight. He emphasized the propriety of his conduct toward the Corinthians because it had been brought into question by his critics. His enemies had been saying that Paul did not really mean what he said, so he affirmed that his present writing was clear and understandable. The Corinthians already knew enough to know his sincerity. They had better opportunity than most to know his character. He had been with them many months. He expressed confidence that when they all stood before their Lord, they would be proud of each other.

■ *Because others were boasting, Paul felt that*
■ *he must engage in this foolish approach to set*
■ *the record straight. Because it had been*
■ *brought into question, Paul emphasized the*
■ *propriety of his conduct toward the*
■ *Corinthians.*

DEPENDABLE PROMISES (1:15–22)

Paul's Consistency (vv. 15–20)

At the end of 1 Corinthians (16:5–7), Paul announced a visit to Corinth after he passed through Macedonia. Later he changed his mind and planned two visits, one going to and one coming from Macedonia. When he learned of the Corinthians hostility toward him, he again changed his plans. He believed a second visit would only bring added pain. The Corinthians thought, or were likely to think, that Paul was wishy-washy. If he were truly inconsistent, then this flaw would extend to his preaching as well. Such an inference was unthinkable to Paul.

Not only was Paul's preaching consistent and positive; it was concerned with these very characteristics in Christ Himself. God has promised salvation to His people, and Christ had fulfilled that promise.

God's Works in the Believer (vv. 21, 22)

Paul introduced this section (1) to affirm his integrity as a messenger of the gospel, and (2) to show that the trustworthiness of his gospel message rested upon the work of God. Paul made it clear to his readers that his faithfulness was not the result of his own accomplishment. Here he revealed four works of God in the life of the believer.

"Firm"

"The word was used in the papyri of making a legal guarantee and appears often in the guarantee clause of a bill of sale" (Fritz Rienecker, *Linguistic Key to the Greek New Testament* [Grand Rapids: Zondervan, 1980], 454).

"A seal on a document in New Testament times identified it and indicated its owner, who would protect it. So too, in salvation the Holy Spirit, like a seal, confirms that Christians are identified with Christ and are God's property, protected by Him" (*The Bible Knowledge Commentary*, Victor Books, 556).

God makes us stand firm (v. 21). The word *firm* means "steadfast" and "secure."

God anoints us (v. 21). This anointing refers to the anointing of the Holy Spirit that takes place at the time of a believer's conversion.

God has sealed us (v. 22). Paul said that God "set his seal of ownership on us."

God has given us his Spirit as a guarantee (v. 22). The presence of God's Spirit in the believer's life witnesses to his inheritance in the kingdom of God and enables the believer to serve God. In this way the Spirit is a "down payment" or *earnest*; a guarantee of what is to come.

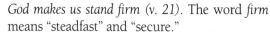

- *In spite of accusations of inconsistency, Paul*
- *showed that the trustworthiness of his gospel*
- *message rests upon the work of God. He*
- *revealed four works of God at work in his life*
- *and ministry that confirmed Paul's own*
- *faithfulness was not the result of his own*
- *accomplishment.*

DETERMINED TO DO NO HARM (1:23–2:4)

"God as My Witness" (1:23)

After his defense of his gospel, Paul returned to the immediate question about his change in plans. This change was to benefit the Corinthians. Paul felt it so important to emphasize this that he was willing to call God as a witness against him if he were not telling the truth. Because he had spoken so strongly, he did not want the Corinthians to think that he was claiming too much authority. He did not see himself as their lord. Rather, he was their fellow worker, and his aim was joy in their lives. Nor did he think they needed an authoritarian leader, for they were firm in the faith.

A Change in Plans (2:1–4)

His decision not to make another visit, then, was to avoid causing pain to the church. His last visit had done this, and Paul saw no reason to repeat the pain. For him, to hurt the believers at Corinth would be to hurt himself. They were his source of joy. If he caused them sorrow, they could not make him glad.

Instead of making a second, painful visit, Paul wrote a painful letter (which some believe is the material included in 2 Cor. 10–13). Even this was difficult for him, and he wanted them to know that he did it out of love to restore the joy that should exist in relationship.

- Paul changed his travel plans to benefit the
- Corinthian congregation. He decided not to
- make another visit to avoid causing further
- pain to the church.

Earnest

This is a word of Semitic origin (possibly Phoenician). It has a common use in the papyri as earnest money in a purchase for a cow or for a wife (a dowry). In the New Testament, the word appears only in 2 Corinthians 1:22 and Ephesians 1:4. "It is a part payment on the total obligation and we use the very expression today, 'earnest money.' It is God, says Paul, who has done all this for us and the Spirit is God's pledge that He is sincere. This earnest of the Spirit in our hearts is the witness of the Spirit that we are God's" (A. T. Robertson, *Word Pictures in the New Testament*, "Epistles of Paul," vol. 4, 214).

QUESTIONS TO GUIDE YOUR STUDY

1. How did Paul's opening greeting differ from that found in the typical hellenistic letter of his day?

2. For what was Paul thankful to God?

3. For the Christian, what is the purpose of suffering? What should be the Christian's attitude toward suffering?

4. Paul revealed four works of God that enable the believer to serve Him. What are they, and what does each do for the believer?

Note: The first four verses of chapter 2 are part of the discussion of chapter 1 and are treated there.

A wrongdoer in the Corinthian congregation had been punished by the majority of the members. Paul was concerned that Satan might gain a foothold in the Corinthian congregation if the offending member was overwhelmed with grief. To prevent this, Paul urged the congregation to reaffirm their love for this person.

HOW TO TREAT A TROUBLEMAKER (2:5–11)

Here Paul began to address the specific problem between himself and the believers at Corinth. He wrote with such tact and restraint that he did not give enough details to provide an adequate explanation of the problem for the modern reader. What we know for certain is that one man had done something to hurt the entire congregation and Paul as well. The most likely explanation is that it was Paul himself who had been wronged by a member who had questioned Paul's authority as an apostle, his integrity, and perhaps even his motives regarding money (2 Cor. 12:14–18).

"My purpose was not to write about who did the wrong or who was wronged. I wrote to you so that in the sight of God you could show how much you really do care for us" (2 Cor. 7:12, NLT).

Paul mentioned this offense in 7:12. In that passage he indicated that he did not want to focus on the wrongdoer or the one hurt. He wanted, instead, to influence the attitude of the congregation. At this point, we may assume that the wrongdoer had been brought to repentance. Paul now urged the congregation to engage in the restoration of this person and, in verse 7, offered his twofold instruction to the Corinthians for doing so.

They were to forgive and comfort the wrongdoer. The Corinthians were to be gracious toward the wrongdoer and take steps in comforting him.

They were to reaffirm their love for the wrongdoer. Paul called on the members of the congregation to reaffirm their love for the wrongdoer. The majority of the church members had already disciplined the offender in some way, and Paul felt that was enough. The next step was for the congregation to forgive this person, lest he be overcome by sorrow.

Paul wanted the Corinthians to know that he joined them in forgiving this person. His purpose in writing the letter of rebuke had been accomplished. He simply wanted to be sure that the Corinthian believers would be obedient to Christ and that the integrity of his ministry was recognized. In forgiving the offender, Paul recognized that Christ was present in the situation and that he himself was seeking the welfare of the church. Not to forgive the offenders was to let Satan win the war after the church had already won the battle.

■ *Paul spoke of the specific problem between*
■ *him and the believers at Corinth. Appar-*
■ *ently, Paul himself had been wronged by a*
■ *member who questioned his authority as an*
■ *apostle, his integrity, and perhaps his*
■ *motives regarding money. Paul's response*
■ *was to call for redemption, not retaliation.*

PAUL AWAITS TITUS (2:12–13)

Paul's pattern in this letter was to state a fact about his personal history and then launch a discussion of some larger idea. Here he

Comfort means "to encourage, to exhort, to urge on." "It is used of the speeches of leaders and of soldiers who urge each other on. It is the word used to send hesitant soldiers and sailors courageously into battle" (Fritz Rienecker, *Linguistic Key to the Greek New Testament* [Grand Rapids: Zondervan, 1980], 456).

"Overwhelmed by excessive sorrow"

The word *overwhelm* is a compound word made up of the preposition "down" and the verb "to swallow." They combine to form a word that means "to swallow down," or "to swallow up completely." This word was used of waves that engulf things and people. Paul was concerned that if the congregation failed to forgive this repentant member, he might drown in his excessive sorrow. A lesson here is that God's people need to be sensitive about when enough punishment is sufficient for an offense.

"Some Satan destroyed through sin, others through the unmeasured sorrow following on repentance for it . . . conquering us with our own weapons."

—Chrysostom

prepared to plunge into an extended discussion of his ministry as an apostle, but his starting point was once again from his personal experience.

Paul came to Troas to preach the gospel and found great opportunity. While in Troas, he awaited the return of Titus. When he did not find Titus, his anxiety about the situation moved him to go on to Macedonia.

- Paul recounted his anxiety while awaiting
- the reply to his "severe" letter to the Corin-
- thians. He journeyed to Troas and ultimately
- Macedonia to learn the results of Titus's
- visit.

GOD'S VICTORY MARCH (2:14–17)

Instead of describing his reunion with Titus, Paul broke into an exclamation of praise for the way God had worked in their ministry. Not until 7:5 did he return to the subject of his trip to Macedonia. There he told how Titus met him in Macedonia with joyful news from Corinth. The thought of that joy seemed to be in Paul's mind as he began his discourse on ministry in verse 14.

The news that the Corinthians had repented of their hard feelings (7:9) and were positive toward Paul (7:7) moved him to rejoice. He portrayed God as a Roman general "who always leads us in triumphal procession in Christ" (v. 14). Paul regarded himself as one taken captive by God, a trophy of His saving power. His missionary journeys were occasions when God led him. And just as burning incense filled the air for the Roman victory parades, Paul's ministry was the aroma of Christ to the people he encountered.

Paul then contrasted this profound view of ministry with the approach taken by some of his critics at Corinth. He described these people as "peddlers" of God's message.

- *The news that the Corinthians had repented*
- *of their hard feelings and were positive*
- *toward Paul, moved him to rejoice at the way*
- *God had worked in his ministry. Paul had*
- *shared the gospel with the Corinthians, not*
- *like a huckster peddling his wares, but with*
- *the sincerity of a God-sent spokesman.*

QUESTIONS TO GUIDE YOUR STUDY

1. What instruction did Paul give the Corinthians for dealing with the wrongdoer in their midst? What does this advice teach us about dealing with troublemakers in today's churches?

2. Why did Paul consider the punishment already dealt to the wrongdoer sufficient? What was his concern about this person? What might we as a church today learn from Paul's concern here?

3. What fueled Paul's anxiety as he awaited the report from Titus?

4. Why was Paul so joyful in vv. 14–17?

Peddler

The word for "peddler" suggests a wine merchant who watered down his product; it could be translated "huckster." They sought their own advantage, neglecting the people and altering the message to make their sales on any terms that would profit them (adapted from David C. George, *2 Corinthians, Galatians, Ephesians,* Layman's Bible Book Commentary [Nashville: Broadman & Holman Publishers, 1979], 22).

"It is curious how hucksters were suspected of corrupting by putting the best fruit on top of the basket" (A. T. Robertson, *Word Pictures in the New Testament,* "Epistles of Paul," vol. 4, 219).

Paul, in contrast to peddlers and hucksters, was a sincere representative of Christ accredited by God Himself.

Paul discussed letters of recommendation (common in Paul's day) and explained that no letters of recommendation were necessary to authenticate his ministry to the Corinthians and his apostleship to the church in Corinth. Also in this chapter, Paul contrasted the ministries of the old and new covenants, proving the superiority of the new.

LIVING LETTER (3:1–3)

Paul had just poured out his heart for what God had done in his ministry. He also contrasted his ministry with others who were not sincere. But he did not want anyone to think he was writing a letter of recommendation for himself. Letters of introduction were common in the early church as Christians traveled about. The troublemakers who had come to Corinth apparently had such letters, and they may have objected that Paul did not have them. Paul, however, had something better. His ministry to the people of Corinth made a direct impression on their lives. They, of all people, did not need anyone to vouch for Paul. They were living proof for all to see that Paul was a true minister.

Letters of Recommendation

"Jewish travelers often carried letters of recommendation indicating that Jewish householders could trust them and give them lodging on their journey. In Greco-Roman society, higher-class patrons would write letters recommending their subordinates" (*The Bible Background Commentary: New Testament*, InterVarsity Press, 496).

- *Some had apparently attacked the legitimacy*
- *of Paul's apostleship toward the Corinthian*
- *church. Paul insisted that he needed no spe-*
- *cial recommendation for his work with the*
- *Corinthian believers. The planting of the*
- *church and the transformation of their lives*
- *were Paul's recommendations for ministry*
- *and apostleship.*

COMPETENT MINISTRY (3:4–6)

Paul was very confident, but his confidence rested with God, not himself. He could not claim authority on his own. He had a sense of competence that came from being a minister of the new covenant, which was the new relationship between God and man created by Christ. A minister who offers such a covenant has a distinct advantage over those who present the old covenant or those who preach a legalistic faith. Such forms of legalism all rest on words and rules with a deadening effect. The new covenant is the work of the Spirit, and He provides the life needed for a new creation.

Paul introduced the contrasts between the covenants here because his critics at Corinth took pride in their Jewish background and because the contrast was a basic feature of his own experience. In Romans 7–8 Paul described how the law had only served to expose his helplessness, while Christ had delivered him and given him new life.

Minister

The word *minister* is an important word for Paul. Either the noun, verb, or broader term "ministry" are found in all of Paul's letters except those to the Thessalonians. It means "servant" and it is the same word Jesus used of Himself as one who came to minister (Mark 10:45). In its various forms it occurs often in 2 Corinthians. In 5:18 we see the "ministry of reconciliation." The word does not describe a special office, either *minister* in the modern professional sense or *deacon* in the sense of a lay officer of the church. Rather, it describes the function of service and the role of a servant.

- *Paul continued to defend his ministry before*
- *some of his detractors. He insisted that his*
- *competency in ministry came from God.*

THE FADING GLORY OF THE LAW (3:7–11)

Paul continued to discuss the superiority of the new covenant to the old covenant. Moses was minister of the old covenant. Paul called it a ministry of death (v. 7) and condemnation (v. 9). This did not mean that the law was evil. To the contrary, God gave it and Paul had been devoted to it. But he knew that it did not bring life. It was provisional and needed to be replaced by something permanent. It was carved on stone (v. 7) and had only external authority. What was needed was a living, spiritual covenant that had inner force in people's lives. The old covenant was given with great splendor and glory. Moses' face shone with the radiance of his encounter with God, but the glow was only temporary.

Paul argued that the new covenant is superior, and he provided several reason for his readers.

1. *It involves the ministry of the Holy Spirit* (v. 8). The Spirit enables people to walk and live in the commandments of God. Paul called the old covenant the "ministry of death."
2. *It brings righteousness* (v. 9). The new covenant is a glorious ministry that brings righteousness. The old covenant condemned people by exposing their sin.
3. *It is permanent* (v. 11). The new covenant is "that which lasts." The old covenant was temporary and had faded.

Contrast Between the Old and New Covenants

OLD COVENANT	NEW COVENANT
Ministry of death	Ministry of the Spirit (life)
Brings condemnation	Brings righteousness
Temporary in nature	Permanent in nature

- *Paul proclaimed that the ministry of the new*
- *covenant is superior to that of Moses because*
- *the new covenant features the ministry of the*
- *Spirit, produces righteousness, and provides*
- *permanence.*

THE LIFE-CHANGING GLORY OF CHRIST (3:12–18)

The minister of the new covenant is in a much better position than was Moses. Moses put a veil over his face because it shone (Exod. 34:33–35). The Exodus account does not specify why he did this, but Paul explained that he did not want the Corinthians to see the fading of the glow of God's glory.

Paul went on to apply the idea of the veil to what happened when the people of Israel read the law in his own day. The lack of God's living presence in their hearts made them unable to see what God wanted to reveal. This "veil" or obstacle is removed when people turn to the Lord. "The Lord"—that is, Christ—"is the Spirit" (v. 17). This does not mean that there is no difference between Christ and the Holy Spirit. Rather, it means that Christ is present and acts in believers through the Spirit.

Paul then contrasted the old covenant with the Spirit's involvement with the new covenant. The Spirit liberates persons so they can receive God's revelation. Paul stated that "where the Spirit of the Lord is, there is freedom." This is what the law lacked. Moses had only the written law and a brief, fading glimpse of glory.

Christ has the life-changing Spirit and an ever-increasing glory. Paul wrote that believers

"Transformed into his likeness"

Christians are not deified but are transformed when they see the image of God in Jesus. The verb "being transformed" is in the present tense, indicating an extended process and emphasizing its progressive nature. The words "ever-increasing glory" are literally "from glory to glory." Christians are transformed into the image of God, as expressed in the life of Jesus, from one stage of glory to a higher stage . . . (portions taken from Fritz Rienecker, *Linguistic Key to the Greek New Testament* [Grand Rapids: Zondervan, 1980], 461).

"are being transformed into his likeness with ever-increasing glory" (v. 18). The word *transformed* is the Greek word *metamorpheo*, from which we get our English word *metamorphosis*.

- Paul contrasted the old covenant with the
- Spirit's involvement with the new covenant.
- Where the life-changing Spirit of the Lord is,
- there is freedom. This is what the law lacked.
- Paul added that believers "are being trans-
- formed into his likeness with ever-increasing
- glory."

QUESTIONS TO GUIDE YOUR STUDY

1. What was the purpose of a letter of recommendation in Paul's day? Why did he insist on not needing one? Upon what did he base the competency of his ministry?
2. Paul contrasted the new and old covenants. Why is the new covenant superior?
3. What happens when a person "turns to" the Lord and removes the "veil" covering his or her heart?
4. How is the believer transformed into the likeness of God?

In light of the ministry that God had entrusted to Paul, he described how he conducted himself to accomplish his mission. He closed the chapter by explaining the content of the gospel.

THE MINISTRY OF LIGHT (4:1–6)

Paul's Appeal to the Conscience (vv. 1, 2)

Paul begins with the conjunction "therefore." Literally, it means "because of this," and it points to Paul's preceding words about the glory of ministry in the new covenant. Because he had such confidence in his gospel and in the mercy of God, Paul could not be discouraged in spite of the many problems he had endured as a minister of the gospel.

Neither did Paul allow his difficulties to pressure him into taking shortcuts in his ministerial duties. Other teachers at Corinth may have seemed to present a more popular approach to the faith. Unfortunately, ministers, like other people, were sometimes tempted to use questionable methods or to water down their message to make it more acceptable to the masses. Paul was determined not to do this. His Lord and his gospel demanded that he be open and truthful at all times and in all things. Paul's appeal was to the conscience, not to lower instincts.

"The God of This Age" (vv. 3–6)

Paul recognized that not everyone would understand and accept the gospel. Some were perishing in unbelief and could not see the light of Christ because they were spiritually blind. Satan is the god of this age, not a true god but one whom people have mistaken for their god. He is a deceiver and works to keep people from

Age

Although sometimes translated "world" in some English versions, this word is literally "age." Here it refers to all that floating mass of thoughts, opinions, maxims, speculations, hopes, impulses, aims, aspirations at any time current in the world" (Fritz Rienecker, *Linguistic Key to the Greek New Testament* [Grand Rapids: Zondervan, 1980], 463).

seeing the truth of the person of Jesus Christ and of God's Word.

This passage is the only place in Scripture where Satan is called "the god of this age." This statement does not mean that God has surrendered control of His world to Satan, but rather that people have used their free will to give him a measure of power in their lives. Satan's corrupt rule is limited to this age only, whereas God's rule is for all ages to come.

Satan's Realm of Control

HIS TITLE	PASSAGE
"The god of this age"	2 Cor. 4:4
"The ruler of the kingdom of the air"	Eph. 2:2
"The prince of this world"	John 12:31

Whereas Satan is a false god, Jesus is the very likeness of God. Paul pointed out that it is Jesus Christ who was the subject of his preaching, not Paul himself. He made it a point to describe himself as a servant of Christ whose concern was the welfare of the Corinthians.

Christ the Light (v. 6)

God has given His people a light in their hearts that comes from His self-revelation through the person of Christ. "Christ shares in God's real being and is a perfect manifestation of that being" (Fritz Rienecker, *Linguistic Key to the Greek New Testament* [Grand Rapids: Zondervan, 1980], 463). Here Paul agreed with the apostle John that those who have encountered Christ have beheld the glory of God (John 1:14, 18; 14:9).

■ *Paul did not allow his difficulties to pressure*
■ *him into taking shortcuts in his ministerial*
■ *duties. He realized that many unbelievers*
■ *were spiritually blinded by Satan, the god of*
■ *this age. However, God causes the light of the*
■ *knowledge of His glory through Christ to*
■ *shine "out of the darkness."*

A TREASURE IN JARS OF CLAY (4:7–12)

In spite of Paul's best efforts, some Corinthians were not impressed. The difference lay in the fact that Paul's experience with the gospel had been quite different from theirs. He had suffered intense persecution, including imprisonment and stoning. The Corinthians had not faced this kind of opposition. Neither had the believers at Corinth faced strong Jewish opposition to the gospel or been pressured to worship Caesar. The church may have been on too good of terms with its culture and environment. Because they understood only internal strife rather than enduring external attacks, it may have been too easy for them to look down on Paul.

Paul devoted this portion of his letter to dealing with their differences in experience.

Believers Are a Treasure (v. 7)

A messenger of the gospel is like a clay jar carrying precious contents. The contents of the jar is the treasure of the gospel. A key point here is that the treasure of the gospel does not receive its value from its container. Rather, it derives its power from God. Paul made it clear that this treasure is something that "we have," that is, all Christians possess it. The contents consist of

Clay Jars

In the ancient world almost everything was stored in clay jars, including treasure. Corinthian pottery was well-known in the ancient world and Paul may have been referring to the small pottery lamps which were cheap and fragile, or he may have been referring to earthenware vases or urns. The point seems to be that the valuable treasure is contained in weak, fragile, valueless containers.

"the knowledge of the glory of God in the face of Christ" (v. 6).

Clay Jars Are Frail (vv. 8–12)

To show how the power of God works in spite of human frailty and weakness, Paul mentioned five crisis situations that can endanger the frail clay jar. Were it not for the strength from a higher power, these clay jars would have failed or broken.

Crisis #1: external pressure (v. 8). An example is the persecution Paul endured for the sake of the gospel. In such situations, clay jars are "not abandoned." Christians are never without a way to endure or escape (1 Cor. 10:13).

Crisis #2: inner perplexity (v. 8). This term means to be perplexed and despondent. It was used in Paul's day of a person who was ruined by creditors and at wit's end.

Crisis #3: interpersonal conflict (v. 8). This describes a person retreating from enemies who are pursuing him. Even in such dire straits, God gives support.

Crisis #4: acute danger (v. 9). The idea here is of one knocked or thrown down with force. This refers to the throwing down of an opponent in wrestling, or striking down another with a sword. A warrior may be wounded and down, but he is not finished. God is still at work even in the midst of defeat and mortal danger.

Crisis #5: impending death. This refers to the process of dying or putting to death. In his missionary journeys, Paul was constantly exposed to death.

- *A messenger of the gospel is like a clay jar*
- *carrying precious contents. The contents of*
- *the jar is the treasure of the gospel. The frail*
- *clay jar is very vulnerable, potentially plac-*
- *ing its contents at risk. To show how the*
- *power of God works in spite of human frailty*
- *and weakness, Paul mentioned five crises*
- *that require God's strength to ensure that the*
- *jars are not broken.*

THE SPIRIT OF FAITH (4:13–15)

Paul quoted the Greek version (the Septuagint) of Ps. 116:10 (NRSV), "I kept my faith, even when I said, 'I am greatly afflicted.'" Like the psalmist, Paul bore witness to a faith that endures suffering. He also had something in common with the Corinthians. He and they would experience resurrection with Christ into the presence of God. Paul's suffering was for their sake, and the grace that flowed through his ministry would bring glory to God. Thus, the frail clay jars through his ministry would bring glory to God. They would prove to be carriers of heavenly treasure.

- *Paul quoted from Ps. 116 to show that he*
- *bore witness to a faith that endures suffering.*
- *He informed the Corinthians that both he*
- *and they would experience resurrection with*
- *Christ. All of this would bring glory to God.*

PREPARATION FOR GLORY (4:16–18)

Paul introduced a series of contrasts to drive home his points.

Paul's hope in Christ prevented him from becoming discouraged: "We do not lose heart" (v. 16). In fact, his inner life was gaining him new strength from God as Paul explained, "We are being renewed day by day." What God had in store for him was beyond description. It was vast and never-ending. "For our light and momentary troubles are achieving for us an eternal glory that far outweighs them all" (v. 17).

1. *The outer nature is wasting away and the inner nature is being renewed.* Although the body perishes, the believer's inner nature is daily renewed by God's power. Paul looked forward to the day when he would be in the presence of God in a resurrected body.

2. *Temporary affliction and eternal glory.* In a fallen world, Christians will suffer afflictions. These temporary afflictions "are achieving" an eternal glory that far outweighs any afflictions that we may experience in this life. The words "are achieving" imply a prolonged process that is worked out completely.

3. *What is seen is temporary and what is not seen is eternal.* Paul was not merely contrasting the visible with the invisible. He was contrasting what we see *now* in this life and *what will be revealed* in the future (e.g., Christ and His kingdom at the Second Coming).

Paul had no visible proof of all this. He based his hope in unseen reality. While visible evidence can only be temporary, the unseen work of God is eternal.

- *The afflictions Paul faced were light in contrast*
- *with the glory God was storing up for him. God*
- *also gave Paul an ability to view events from an*
- *eternal rather than a temporal viewpoint.*

QUESTIONS TO GUIDE YOUR STUDY

1. What did Paul mean when he called Satan the "power of this age"?

2. What was Paul conveying by his analogy of a treasure in clay jars?

3. What was Paul's point in his discussion of the five crisis situations that endanger frail clay jars?

4. Paul made a series of contrasts relating to the believer's future glory. What are these contrasts and what truths do they convey?

In this chapter Paul continued his topic of ministry. For him, ministry radiated with the hope of the resurrection. His discussion here revealed Paul's view about life after death. Also in this chapter, Paul defined his motive and message for ministry, both of which are rooted in the work of Christ on the cross.

A highlight is one of the apostle's major themes of his letter—reconciliation. God had given Paul a ministry of reconciliation to proclaim the gospel to all people, and Christ's love compelled him to endure unbelievable hardships in carrying out his mission.

AN EARTHLY TENT AND A HEAVENLY HOME (5:1–5)

As Paul compared his present, human frailty with the coming glory of resurrection, he returned his readers to a prominent theme from his first letter to the Corinthians (1 Cor. 15)—the change that will take place in the believer's body. For all human beings, the present, physical life will someday end. Paul likened our bodies to "tents" that will be taken down so that we can go home to our permanent houses. The Christian need not fear dismantling the tent because those in Christ have another, more permanent abode.

This heavenly dwelling, created by God, can also be compared to a garment. By striking the body-tent, death threatens to leave a person unprotected and vulnerable. But moving into the heavenly dwelling wraps the believer in a new covering of life. Although we naturally experience anxiety as we face death, we may

Tent

Paul likened the believer's body to a tent. The verb used here that is translated as "dissolved" or "destroyed" is the same word used for "striking down" a tent. Those on a journey strike their tents in order to move to the next destination.

find strength in the promise of new life. God prepares us for this event by giving us the Holy Spirit as an advance assurance of resurrection and heavenly life.

■ *Paul's ministry radiated with the hope of*
■ *receiving the resurrection body at Christ's*
■ *return. He considered his present possession*
■ *of the Holy Spirit to be a deposit assuring*
■ *him of future victory.*

AT HOME OR AWAY (5:6–11)

Because Paul's security was in God, he could be confident even in the face of death. For the believer in Christ, earthly life in this present body is like a trip away from home. Death becomes a return home. Paul realized that being at home with God would be best, but he gave himself totally to life and to his ministry in the present by exercising faith and by doing what pleased God.

Whether on earth or in heaven, Paul knew that he was responsible to God for what he did in this life. He shifted his mind from the visions of death as a homecoming to the concept of death as judgment.

Paul saw Christ as the Judge of *all*. All, including Paul himself, must stand before the judgment seat. Paul clearly taught that Christians are saved by grace, through faith, not by their own accomplishments (Eph. 2:8–9). But he also knew that believers are saved to do God's work (v. 10). When they appear before the Lord, some of their works will be seen to be unworthy. Others will receive His approval. This did not shake Paul's confidence in his relationship

Judgment Seat

In Bible times, a *judgment seat* was a raised platform or bench. Pontius Pilate occupied a judgment seat while deliberating the accusations made against Jesus (Matt. 27:19; cp. Acts 18:12). In Rom. 14:10 and 2 Cor. 5:10, the judgment seat of Christ is a theological concept, emphasizing that individuals are accountable to the Lord for their lives and must one day face Him in judgment.

with Christ, but it made him aware of the need to live responsibly.

■ *Paul's' knowledge that he ultimately would be*
■ *"at home with the Lord" filled him with a desire*
■ *to please God through his present actions. It is*
■ *important to live responsibly, for all will be*
■ *made accountable at the judgment seat.*

THE MOTIVE AND THE MESSAGE (5:12–15)

Paul's Motive (v. 12)

Paul may have been speaking of his evangelistic ministry when he said, "We persuade men." But because he had been criticized by his opponents as being insincere, it was more likely that he was referring to his efforts to persuade the Corinthians of his sincerity. In response to this criticism, Paul revealed that he was constantly aware of God's purpose and judgment. It was characteristic of Paul always to be mindful of God's seeing and knowing his every act.

Paul was not bragging. Rather, he was trying to meet a need in the lives of his friends. The critics had raised questions in their minds. They put the emphasis on their outward standing in the church; Paul placed it on inner standing in relation to God. Motive is what truly counts, and God knew Paul's motives. The Corinthians needed to be reassured, and they needed to have ammunition to counter the critics. Any doubt at this point would injure the effectiveness of Paul's message. This he wanted to avoid at all costs. Chapters 10–12 provide extensive details about Paul's concern at this point.

Paul's Message (vv. 13–15)

There is some question about the interpretation of verse 13. Was Paul being accused of indulging in excessive ecstatic experience? Many interpreters take it that way. However, a closer study of the Corinthian situation makes it more likely that Paul had refrained from public displays of such experiences (1 Cor. 14:19). His critics, on the other hand, had joined in this popular activity at Corinth and thought Paul unspiritual because of his restraint. He answered that he did know what it meant to be "beside himself" with ecstasy, but this was only between him and God. In his relation with the Corinthian believers, he found it more helpful to be in his right mind. This twofold concern with the glory of God and the good of the people is a constant theme of his ministry.

Verses 14–21 provide us with one of the most important statements of the gospel message in the New Testament. In these verses Paul emphasized that the controlling factor of his ministry was the love of Christ as seen in His death on the cross. Paul was deeply influenced by Christ's love. It was from his Lord that he learned such dedication. Paul wrote that "Christ's love compels us." Paul did not have in mind the impulse that sent him on his mission, but rather the restraint that kept him focused on the cross and from seeking his own advantage.

The word for "compel" has the sense of pressure that confines and restricts. Such a total commitment to the good of others prevented Paul from doing something that might falsify the gospel or hinder his Christian growth or those to whom he was ministering.

"Compel"

Writing of the usage of this word in the New Testament, Greek scholar A. T. Robertson tells us this word means "to hold together, to press the ears together (Acts 7:57), to press on every side (Luke 8:45), to hold oneself to (Acts 18:5), to be pressed (Luke 12:50; Phil. 1:23). So here Paul's conception of Christ's love for him holds him together to his task whatever men think or say" (*Word Pictures in the New Testament*, "Epistles of Paul," vol. 4, 230).

In verse 15 the *motive* of Paul's ministry and his *message* are viewed as the same, for both flowed from Christ's work on the cross. The death of Christ was the most important fact in Paul's thinking. It affected all people by making possible the most radical change in their lives. Paul saw Christ as the second Adam (Rom. 5:14–17), God's new beginning in the creation of humanity. As such, Christ is the representative of the human race. What happened to Him happens to all humanity in some sense. Those who accept their unity with Christ by faith take part in the death He died for them.

Death to sin and resurrection in order to embrace new life becomes the pattern in the lives of Christians. They no longer live to serve themselves. Instead, they live for Christ and others. This is more than mere acceptance of an idea; it is participation in a new reality. Paul saw his task as making all persons aware of this new possibility and enlisting them to experience it. Paul used the word *all* prominently in verses 14 and 15, which indicates the scope of his missionary goal.

Christ's Death and the Believer*

PURPOSE	PASSAGE
That we might live *through* Him	1 John 4:9
That we might live *with* Him	1 Thess. 5:10
That we might live *for* Him	2 Cor. 5:15

*(Developed from material in Warren Wiersbe, *Wiersbe's Expository Outlines in the New Testament* [Wheaton, Ill.: Victor Books, 1992], 489.)

■ *God had given Paul a ministry of reconciliation*
■ *to proclaim the gospel to all people. Christ's*
■ *love compelled him to carry out that ministry.*

THE NEW HAS COME (5:16–21)

Paul's critics valued persons on the basis of outward appearances and superficial signs. They judged Paul and themselves "from a wordly point of view" (literally "according to the flesh"). Paul told the Corinthians that such evaluations are sub-Christian. To take a strictly human point of view is to miss what God is doing.

From the point of his conversion on, Paul did not evaluate others merely in terms of their human characteristics. He was most concerned with their hearts and the work of the Spirit in their lives. As a new person, he saw with new eyes. This led to his overwhelming concern for others.

In verse 17, "therefore" points back to Paul's words about Christ's death for all and all dying with Him (vv. 4–15). With His resurrection from the dead, the human race gained a new beginning with God. All who unite with Christ by faith become part of this new creation. They are "in Christ," a phrase Paul used constantly throughout his letters to describe his relationship with Christ. It implies that those who exercise faith in Christ enter into a real, personal union with Him. In verse 17 Paul told his readers that two life–changing things take place:

1. *"Old things are passed away"* (KJV). A new outlook takes hold of the believer. Although the old persists throughout this life, the *new* will be culminated at the resurrection.

Reconcile

Paul uses a Greek word here that is used only six times in the New Testament. And Paul is the only New Testament writer to use this word. In five of the six uses, Paul dealt with the relationship between God and human beings. In 1 Corinthians, Paul used this verb when describing the reconciliation between a husband and wife. Even though it is used so infrequently, it carries a lot of theological weight. It communicates the action God has taken which makes possible a peaceful relation between God and man.

2. *"All things are become new"* (KJV). Believers have already begun their participation in the new creation. The new creation is God's doing and will not be fully revealed until the new heaven and the new earth appear and Christians receive their resurrection bodies. But for those who are in Christ, the new order has already begun.

Such a new creation requires that the hostility and separation between man and God be ended. The need for reconciliation implies that a state of enmity has existed due to sin. In his discussion of reconciliation, Paul emphasized what God does for humanity to overcome their hostility toward Him. He indicated that "God was reconciling the world to himself in Christ" (v. 19).

Paul went on to make a forceful appeal in verse 20. The reconciliation of man to God has been accomplished in Christ, but it must be known and accepted to become effective. This has become Paul's ministry.

God's general appeal comes to persons through messengers like Paul, who are here called "ambassadors." Paul saw himself as the direct representative of God in foreign, hostile territory, inviting former enemies to come into God's family.

To reinforce his appeal, Paul restated the means and results of reconciliation (v. 21). Reconciliation between God and man is made possible by Christ's remedy for sin. "Made him to be sin" (v. 21, NRSV) means at least that God the Son bore the consequences of sin. But it is a daring phrase that may mean much more. In some mysterious sense, the sinless Christ became identified with our sin so we could become identified with His righteousness. As a result of this, those who are in Christ by faith "become the righteousness of

God" (v. 21)—that is, they receive the benefits of God's righteousness. They take on the characteristics of Christ as He takes on their former characteristics as sinners. This is not simply a label of righteousness. They become righteous as they are transformed into the image of Christ.

The Doctrine of Reconciliation

CHRIST'S WORK	ASPECT OF RECONCILIATION
His death and resurrection	The *means* of reconciliation
His atonement	The *basis* of reconciliation
His incarnation	The *channel* of reconciliation

- *With Christ's resurrection from the dead, the*
- *human race gained a new beginning with*
- *God. All who unite with Christ by faith*
- *become part of this new creation. In order for*
- *this to be possible, God reconciled the world*
- *to Himself through Christ by having His Son*
- *bear the consequences of the sin of all man-*
- *kind. Those who are in Christ receive the*
- *benefits of God's righteousness.*

QUESTIONS TO GUIDE YOUR STUDY

1. What did Paul tell us about his view of the afterlife in this chapter?
2. What was Paul's motive for ministry? What was his message?
3. What is the "new creation"? Who participates in it?
4. What does it mean to be reconciled to God? What does this involve? How is it possible?

Ambassador

The Greeks used this word to describe an important official in the Roman Empire. Roman provinces that were peaceful were under the direct control of the emperor and his representative on the scene, called an *ambassador*. This person was the direct, personal representative of the emperor. When a country was in the process of becoming a Roman province, the senate would send ten ambassadors to arrange the terms of peace. Thus, an ambassador was one who brought former enemies into the family of Rome. (From David C. George, *2 Corinthians, Galatians, Ephesians,* Layman's Bible Book Commentary [Nashville: Broadman & Holman Publishers, 1979], 32.)

Chapter 6 continues the thought of 5:20. From his side of the relationship, Paul was reconciled to the Corinthians. He had nothing against them. If there was any blockage in the relationship, it rested with the Corinthians.

SERVANTS OF GOD IN EVERY WAY (6:1–10)

Paul's Appeal for Reconciliation (vv. 1–3)

In this section of his letter Paul made an appeal for reconciliation with the Corinthian congregation. Paul was cooperating with God in a partnership of preaching. Reconciliation requires both divine action and communication by a human witness. The plea to the Corinthians was that they not receive the grace of God in vain. Some of them might not have responded in faith to the message. More likely, Paul was telling the Corinthians to make use of the grace they had received. Don't let it go to waste.

Instead of this, he reminded them of the promise in Isa. 49:8: "In the time of my favor I will answer you, and in the day of salvation I will help you." Paul used this verse to emphasize the urgency of his appeal. The day of salvation had already come. The blessings of the kingdom were theirs. The present moment was the time to trust fully in God's redemption.

Paul again emphasized the positive nature of his ministry. Aware that some found fault with his work, he did not yield to their criticism. He was confident that he had done nothing to hinder their faith. To the contrary, he had done everything as a servant of God. Therefore, all his experiences had worked to commend the gospel.

Endurance

- *In this section of his letter Paul made an*
- *appeal for reconciliation with the Corin-*
- *thians. He used Isa. 49:8 to emphasize the*
- *urgency of his appeal. Now is the time to*
- *trust fully in God's redemption.*

Paul's Sufferings (vv. 4, 5)

Paul then listed his sufferings as he did earlier in 4:8, 9. He cited the very things that made him unimpressive to his critics as ways of commending the gospel. His endurance throughout these hardships bore witness to the patient suffering of Christ. "Through great endurance" (NRSV) seems to be the umbrella heading under which he listed nine kinds of suffering in three groups

The first set of difficulties were the conditions under which Paul worked. They describe increasing degrees of difficulty.

Troubles. This is a much-used word in the New Testament. It describes the pressures or crushing burdens of life.

Hardships. Literally, this means "necessities" or "things that cannot be avoided."

Distresses. This word means "a place that is too narrow." It describes those situations in life when there seems to be no way of escape.

The second triplet of troubles described the attacks Paul suffered from his opponents.

Beatings. This refers to stripes from whips and rods with which Paul was beaten by his persecutors.

Imprisonments. "Imprisonments" refer to the times when Paul was actually put in jail.

"Endurance" is one of the key words of the New Testament. It is a compound word made up of the preposition "under" and the verb "to remain." It means "a remaining under" (*Vine's Complete Expository Dictionary of Old and New Testament Words* [Nashville: Thomas Nelson, 1996], 200).

Paul had already used the verb form in 1:6 as he described the endurance of suffering which he and the Corinthians had in common. The word *endurance* occurs throughout Paul's writings, especially Romans and 2 Corinthians. It refers to constant strength under difficulty. Jesus gave it great emphasis (Luke 21:19; Mark 13:13; Matt. 10:22; 24:13). Early Christian writers often described it as the chief Christian virtue. It does not mean passive acceptance of difficulty but the transformation of trouble into victory. In modern terms it could be described as coping successfully with life. (See David C. George, *2 Corinthians, Galatians, Ephesians,* Layman's Bible Book Commentary [Nashville: Broadman & Holman Publishers, 1979], 33.)

Paul knew the inside of prisons in Philippi, Jerusalem, Caesarea, Rome, and probably many other places before his life was over.

A. T. Robertson notes that each of these words "carries a story that can be filled in from Paul's own life."

Riots. This refers to disorders and probably referred to the mob violence which Paul often encountered.

This third set includes the hardships Paul accepted in doing the work of a missionary.

Hard work. This describes work to the point of exhaustion. It was a term Paul often used to describe his work, and it is almost synonymous with the Christian life in the New Testament.

Sleepless nights. Because of duty, discomfort, or danger, Paul spent some sleepless nights. These were times of prayer, witness, and even singing (Acts 16:25, and the entire chapter, where Paul's experience in prison at Philippi illustrates this whole list of difficulties).

Hunger. This is going without food because either time or money is lacking. It probably does not mean fasting for religious purposes. Like Jesus and His disciples, Paul sometimes had no "chance to eat" (Mark 6:31). Paul's response to these sufferings turned defeat into triumph.

Paul's Sufferings for the Gospel

WORK CONDITIONS	Troubles Hardships Distresses
ATTACKS FROM OPPONENTS	Beatings Imprisonments Riots
HARDSHIPS OF A MISSIONARY	Hard work Sleepless nights Hunger

Paul's Commendable Features (vv. 6, 7)
Paul next listed features of his ministry by which he commended himself as a minister of the

gospel. He referred to these as his "weapons of righteousness" (v. 7).

Purity. This feature describes the clean heart and clean hands necessary to carry the message of the gospel. It describes moral purity and integrity.

Knowledge. This includes not only understanding of the faith, but also insight into people and common sense about what to do.

Forbearance. This is patience with people and control of one's temper.

Kindness. A feature that refers to a sweet and gracious spirit that avoids harming others.

The Holy Spirit. Although not a quality, the Holy Spirit is the source of all these qualities and the One who gives needed wisdom and skill for ministry. The phrase here might better be translated "a spirit that is holy" or "holiness of spirit."

Genuine love. This is love without any pretense. It is the kind of love God shows.

Truthful speech. This phrase literally reads "by the word of truth" or "the declaration of the truth," and may refer to the preaching of the gospel or to truthfulness in general.

The power of God. This is the ability and authority of the one who sent him to do his work. This is a basic theme of the entire letter as Paul contrasted God's strength with his own weakness. To conclude his list, Paul testified that his equipment for ministry was complete. He had "weapons of righteousness" which were both offensive (the sword was held in the right hand) and defensive (the left hand held the shield).

The Two-Sided Nature of Ministry (vv. 8–10)

In these three verses Paul gave his readers nine contrasting pairs of characteristics that describe the two-sided nature of the ministry. There are many negative factors, but each is outweighed by the positive. Just as the experience of Christ includes both cross and resurrection, the Christian life is full of shadows that witness to the light all around.

Ministry's Contrasting Natures

NEGATIVE SIDE	POSITIVE SIDE
Dishonor	Glory
Bad report	Good report
Imposters	Genuine ministers
Unknown	Well-known
Dying	Living
Beaten	Not yet killed
Sorrowful	Always rejoicing
Poor	Making many rich
Having nothing	Possessing everything

Dishonor . . . glory. This term was used to describe the loss of rights as a citizen. But as a citizen of the kingdom, Paul had a higher honor than this world bestows.

Bad report . . . good report. This is the way many thought of Paul, but with God and God's people his reputation was entirely different.

Imposters . . . genuine ministers. Paul and his fellow missionaries were looked upon as imposters, a word meaning a wandering deceiver or seducer. To those who could recognize it, though, their message was truth itself.

Unknown . . . well-known. Paul's enemies considered him an unknown, but he was well-known by those who received the gospel from him.

Dying . . . living. Paul and his associates were constantly in danger of dying, but they were more fully alive than most. Although they were punished or disciplined, it was never such as to bring death.

Sorrowful . . . always rejoicing. Paul had ample reason to be sorrowful, but nothing could take away his joy.

Poor . . . making many rich. Although poor in terms of earthly wealth, Paul could share the true wealth of the Spirit with all who would receive it.

Having nothing . . . possessing everything. Paul had committed himself to a life of having nothing, but in Christ everything belonged to him.

> *Paul presented a section rich with lists and paradoxes. His endurance throughout hardships bore witness to the patient suffering of Christ. While he waged the battle of the ministry, using the "weapons of righteousness," he remained Christlike in his conduct and character.*

AN APPEAL TO THE HEART (6:11–13)

Now that Paul had spoken to his friends in such bold terms, he paused to ask for their response. He had been completely open with them. He had opened his heart and had offered love to all who would respond. They, however, had not been so open. The problem had been

"We have spoken freely to you"

This phrase is literally "Our mouth is open to you." It means "I am speaking to you frankly, with an open heart, hiding nothing" (Fritz Rienecker, *Linguistic Key to the Greek New Testament* [Grand Rapids: Zondervan, 1980], 473).

"The similar expression, 'He opened his mouth [and taught them]' is often used of Jesus in the Gospels (e.g., Matt. 5:2; 13:35) and reflects a common Hebraic idiom meaning simply 'he spoke.' However, Paul's expression, our mouth is open to you, is a Greek idiom denoting candour, or straightforward speech. By adding, our heart is wide, Paul affirms that there is plenty of room for the Corinthians in his affections" (Colin Kruse, *The Second Epistle of Paul to the Corinthians*, Tyndale New Testament Commentaries [Grand Rapids: Eerdmans, 1987], 135).

"Do not plow with an ox and a donkey yoked together" (Deut. 22:10).

their attitude, not any unwillingness on his part. Now he asked them as he would have asked his own children, "We have spoken freely to you, Corinthians, and opened wide our hearts to you. . . . open wide your hearts also" (vv. 11, 13).

- Paul had opened his heart to all who would
- respond. The Corinthians, however, had not
- been so open to Paul. Now he asked them as
- he would have asked his own children,
- "Open wide your hearts also."

PAUL CAUTIONS AGAINST COMPROMISE (6:14–7:1)

In the middle of his appeal for open hearts, Paul switched gears to discuss the dangers of Christians getting too involved with pagan idol worshipers. Some think this passage was originally part of another letter to Corinth, perhaps the one mentioned in 1 Corinthians 5:9–13. But that letter clearly dealt with immoral Christians. This passage obviously refers to unbelievers. The unequal yoking may refer to Deut. 22:10.

Turning to the Old Testament Scriptures to make his point, Paul cited Isa. 52:11, where the prophet called the Israelites to leave Babylon with its spiritual uncleanness and return to the land of divine promise. Paul also pointed to other Old Testament passages (2 Sam. 7:8, 14; Isa. 43:6; Jer. 31:9) that show God's people are in a special relationship with the world.

- *Paul suspected that the block in their rela-*
- *tionship was brought about by the Corin-*
- *thians' love of the world. He pointed out that*
- *the light cannot be a part of the darkness.*
- *Christians must not be bound to unbelievers*
- *in a way that will affect their moral purity.*

QUESTIONS TO GUIDE YOUR STUDY

1. As Paul appealed to the Corinthians to reconcile with him, he quoted Isa. 49:8. Why did he select this verse from the Old Testament?
2. What is the point of Paul's recounting his sufferings in the ministry of the gospel?
3. Was Paul ready for reconciliation from the Corinthians? What step had he taken? What step did the Corinthians have to take?
4. Paul suspected that the Corinthians had a love for the world. What key point did he make?

How is the command not to be unequally yoked apply? James A. Davis says, "Clearly all association is not forbidden, and so it is probably best to understand Paul's injunction here to prohibit only those relationships in which the degree of association entails an inevitable compromise with Christian standards of conduct" (*Evangelical Commentary on the Bible,* Baker Book House, p. 990).

Christians in today's society need this reminder to keep their lives clean and to live in dedication to God just as they did in pagan Corinth of Paul's day.

In this chapter Paul brought his conversation with the Corinthians to a climax. He renewed his appeal to the Corinthians to open their hearts to him. Paul's concern turned to joy when Titus brought the good news that the Corinthians wanted to be reconciled with Paul.

PAUL CONTINUES HIS APPEAL (7:2–4)

The mood is one of affirmation and joy. Like an evangelist pressing his invitation, Paul said, "Make room for us in your hearts" (v. 2). The issues had been dealt with. There was no longer reason to harbor hard feelings. But Paul knew that broken relationships take time to mend. So he spoke very tenderly to his flock. Reminding them that he had done nothing to hurt them, he also let them know that he was not criticizing them for the strain in their relationship.

Paul's own heart was open to the Corinthians, and he asked them to do the same. Any restrictions in the relationship with Paul from here on would rest with the Corinthians. In verse 2 Paul made three statements that asserted his integrity and built a bridge to the Corinthians.

"Make room in your hearts"

The Greek word used here means "to provide a place for, make room for." It is an imperative form of the verb, indicating that Paul was making a strong appeal to the wills of the Corinthian believers. Paul "wishes no further tightness of heart in them. He makes this plea to all, even the stubborn minority" (A. T. Robertson, *Word Pictures in the New Testament*, "Epistles of Paul," vol. 4, 238).

1. *"We have wronged no one."* To wrong someone has to do with treating someone unjustly or injuriously.

2. *"We have corrupted no one."* To corrupt another is to ruin that person in the areas of money, morals, or doctrine.

3. *"We have exploited no one."* To exploit someone is to take advantage of that person for personal gain or to defraud for the purpose of gain.

Paul insisted to the Corinthians that he was not guilty of any of the above offenses.

The important point is in verse 3. Paul wanted to be in their hearts because they were in his. He was willing to die for them and did not want to live without them. In verse 4 Paul affirmed his friends by making statements of confidence and pride in them:

- "I have great confidence in you;"
- "I take great pride in you."

In spite of the suffering he had experienced for them, he felt only joy and comfort.

■ *Paul asked the Corinthians to "make room*
■ *for us in your hearts." Knowing that broken*
■ *relationships have to be mended slowly with*
■ *love, Paul spoke very tenderly to his flock.*
■ *He reminded them that he had done nothing*
■ *to hurt them and let them know that he was*
■ *not criticizing them for the strain in their*
■ *relationship.*

COMFORTING NEWS FROM CORINTH (7:5–16)

The Crisis Is Resolved (vv. 5–7)

At the height of his expression of joy, Paul began to explain how the change had come about. He had already mentioned his anxious waiting for Titus to return from Corinth (2:12, 13). Now he finished the story. He had suffered acute distress. On the outside, opponents of the gospel resisted him. On the inside, he was concerned about the problems at Corinth. What really saved him from this crisis was the comfort he had received from God. It had

Titus

Titus was a Gentile companion of Paul, and he may have been converted through Paul's ministry. He was the recipient of the New Testament letter bearing his name. He was overseer or bishop of the church at Crete. Paul entrusted him with the delicate task of delivering Paul's severe letter (2 Cor. 2:1–4) to Corinth and correcting problems with the church there. Titus's genuine concern and even-handed dealing with the Corinthians contributed to his success, which he reported in person to Paul. The apostle responded by writing 2 Corinthians, which Titus probably delivered.

come, as spiritual help so often does, through human means. Titus returned at last, and he brought good news.

No Regrets (vv. 8–11)

One of Paul's concerns had been the harsh letter ("severe" letter) he had sent them. Was it too strong? Would they be crushed? For a while he was sorry he had written it, but no longer. Now he knew it provoked only a temporary grief, one that led them to repent. Because this godly grief had led to a change for the better, neither he nor they had any cause to regret it. This process was the opposite of the world's grief over evil, which was despair with no hope of change. Because of their strong desire for change, the Corinthians had proved that things were right again. His letter and its results had helped the Corinthians to realize how much Paul meant to them.

Paul's Confidence in the Corinthians (vv. 12–16)

Titus, as well as Paul, was relieved at the way things had turned out. He had heard from Paul that the Corinthians were really all right, but he was gratified to find that the Corinthians had lived up to Paul's high estimation of them. Paul was glad they had justified his optimism. Titus then shared Paul's love for them, and Paul was filled with all joy and confidence.

■ *Paul rejoiced when Titus told him that God*
■ *had used his strong words to bring about*
■ *repentance and a desire for reconciliation*
■ *from the believers at Corinth. Paul affirmed*
■ *his unchanged devotion toward the Corin-*
■ *thians and expressed confidence in them.*

QUESTIONS TO GUIDE YOUR STUDY

1. What was Paul's appeal in verse 2? Why did he make it?
2. Paul made three statements to defend his integrity. What did these statements accomplish for Paul and the Corinthians?
3. What news did Titus bring from Corinth? What was Paul's response?
4. Why did Paul not regret that he had sent the Corinthians such a harsh letter?

Chapters 8 and 9 provide the most extensive teaching on stewardship found in the New Testament. They also show Paul's brilliant leadership as a missionary statesman.

A GRACIOUS WORK (8:1–7)

The Example of the Macedonian Churches (vv. 1–5)

Because Jerusalem was a major city and a religious center, it attracted many poor people. Many of these impoverished people had become Christians. To compound this problem, Jewish persecution of Christians had increased the poverty of the churches in Palestine. Then, to make matters worse, famine struck the region.

The Macedonian churches included those in Philippi, Thessalonica, and Berea.

In response to this emergency, Paul urged his missionary churches to give an offering to be sent to their Jewish brothers. This gracious work would reveal to the Jews the depth of Christian concern among the Gentiles and remind the Gentiles of their spiritual debt to the Jews who had shared God's revelation with them.

Paul began his appeal to the Corinthians by sharing the example set by the churches of Macedonia. These churches had suffered persecution for their faith. This persecution had affected them financially. Yet they contributed even beyond what they were able to the offering for the Christians in Jerusalem and greater Palestine. Paul wrote, "They gave themselves first to the Lord and then to us in keeping with God's will" (v. 5).

Paul explained this concept in Phil. 2:7, where he wrote that Jesus "made himself nothing" for the sake of mankind.

Paul Urges the Corinthians to Respond (vv. 6,7)

In light of this example, Paul urged the Corinthians to respond because they had not suffered persecution as had the Macedonians. As a result, they should be able to do even more: "See that you also excel in this grace of giving" (v. 7).

- *As incentive for completing the collection of*
- *funds, Paul commended to the Corinthians*
- *the unselfish example of the Macedonian*
- *churches. These churches sacrificed for the*
- *purpose of meeting the needs of their fellow*
- *believers in Palestine.*

THE WHY AND HOW OF GIVING (8:8–15)

The Example of Jesus (vv. 8–9)

Paul did not want the Corinthians to think he was ordering them to give. He wanted them to be motivated by the examples of others because they already had a genuine Christian love. This led him to the very heart of the stewardship motive—the gift of God in Christ.

Paul wrote, "For you know the grace of our Lord Jesus Christ, that though he was rich, yet for your sakes he became poor" (v. 9). Jesus willingly gave Himself, emptying Himself of His divine wealth.

Guideline for Giving (vv. 10–15)

The guideline for giving is "according to your means" (v. 11). A person with much should give much; a person with little should give what is possible. The goal Paul had in mind was equality of needs being met among the Christian churches.

The event described in Philippians 2:5–8 is known as the *kenosis*, derived from the Greek word for "empty" (*kenoo*). In this passage we read that Christ "emptied himself, divested himself of his privileges" (William F. Arndt and F. Wilbur Gingrich, *A Greek-English Lexicon of the New Testament* [Chicago: U. of Chicago Press, 1957], 429). Christ gave up the appearance of divinity and took on the form of a slave.

"Of what did Christ empty Himself? Not of His divine nature. That was impossible. He continued to be the Son of God. There has arisen a great controversy on this word, a *kenosis* doctrine. Undoubtedly Christ gave up His environment of glory. He took upon Himself limitation of place and knowledge and of power, though still on earth retaining more of these than any mere man. It is here that men should show restraint and modesty, though it is hard to believe that Jesus limited Himself by error of knowledge and certainly not by error of conduct. He was without sin, though tempted as we are" (A. T. Robertson, *Word Pictures in the New Testament*, "Epistles of Paul," vol. 4, 444).

In verse 15 Paul quoted Exod. 16:18: "He who gathered much did not have too much, and he who gathered little did not have too little." The Israelites were not permitted to hoard excess manna, but neither was anyone left without enough.

■ *Paul referred to the example of Jesus'*
■ *self-giving. His intent in urging the Corin-*
■ *thians to take part in the offering was to*
■ *allow their "plenty" to offset the "poverty" of*
■ *the Jewish Christians in Jerusalem.*

THE CORINTHIANS AS HELPERS IN GIVING (8:16–24)

Paul also let the Corinthians know that Titus shared his pastoral concern for them. He was not carrying out Paul's instructions; he was leading them in the fund-raising effort because he wanted to do it. This effort was not only to help the Jewish Christians at Jerusalem; Titus was doing it out of concern for the Corinthians.

Paul mentioned two others who were coming to Corinth with Titus. There are at least three reasons for this.

It was social. Christ's ministers enjoy companionship in service, and the Corinthians would enjoy fellowship with these men.

It was strategic. These men were designated by the churches to share in the work of fundraising.

It was precautionary. Paul did not want anyone to suspect him or Titus of wrongdoing in handling money.

Paul did not name the two helpers. It may be that they were not yet known by those at Corinth. Both were Christians with some reputation. One was known for his preaching, and the other was recognized for his earnestness.

Paul closed this chapter by challenging the Corinthians to prove their love to him and to the two trusted helpers and their churches.

■ *Paul made wise, honest plans for receiving*
■ *and transporting the collection to Jerusalem*
■ *so no one could accuse him of dishonesty.*

QUESTIONS TO GUIDE YOUR STUDY

1. According to Paul, in addition to helping meet the financial needs of believers in Jerusalem, what would this gracious act of giving accomplish within the Christian community?

2. Why were the Macedonian believers an example for the Corinthians? How did Paul expect them to respond?

3. What were Paul's guidelines for giving?

4. Why did Paul enlist helpers to aid Titus?

In this chapter Paul continued to deal with the collection for needy believers in Jerusalem. In this discussion Paul explained his theology of giving, including guidelines and features of Christian giving.

PLANNING FOR A WILLING GIFT (9:1–5)

Christians often need help to move from the point of good intentions to action.

Paul knew that the Corinthians were willing and ready to give an offering. He did not need to inform or persuade them. But he did see the need to encourage them.

Because recent problems at Corinth had slowed the offering effort to a virtual standstill, Paul renewed the effort in order to ensure that the task was accomplished. The urgency for moving ahead was dictated, in part, by the time schedule, the need to coordinate the collection effort with other churches, and with Paul's travel plans.

Previously Paul had used the example of the Corinthians to inspire the Macedonians, just as he now used the Macedonians' generosity to inspire the Corinthians. He stated this to remind them that they had a responsibility to live up to. He also wanted to give them enough time to act freely and avoid the pressure of a last-minute drive.

- *Paul explained features about the proper*
- *manner of giving to the needy believers at*
- *Jerusalem. Paul asked the Corinthians for a*
- *generous offering rather than a grudging*
- *donation.*

PAUL'S THEOLOGY OF GIVING (9:6–15)

Guidelines for Giving (vv. 6, 7)

Paul challenged the Corinthians about the spirit in which they needed to make the gift. They should give it bountifully. Paul set forth the principle of planting and harvest and applied it to the entire Christian faith, making several points about the proper manner of giving:

- Generous giving yields generous results.
- Each person should give as his or her heart determines.
- Each person should contribute cheerfully to the gift.

Giving and the Grace of God (vv. 8–11)

In the act of giving, the believer's inner attitude is as important to God as the outward gift. Paul based Christian giving on the biblical understanding of God. If God is a miser, then we need to hang on to and even hoard what we have. But the Bible teaches that God is a generous provider. Everything has its source in Him, and He will continue to supply our needs.

The Christian's Ministry of Giving (vv. 12–15)

Paul described a balance of grace somewhat like the balance of nature. He identified these results of the ministry of giving.

In verse 9 Paul quoted Ps. 112:9: "He has scattered abroad his gifts to the poor." Because He "scatters abroad" and gives gifts "to the poor," God's people can both trust Him to be generous and follow His example.

Giving supplies the needs of God's people (v. 12). As long as each member of the system is functioning properly, the needs of everyone are met. People give to God by giving to one another. The giver is strengthened, the recipient is helped, and God is glorified.

Giving causes God's people to overflow with thanksgiving to God (v. 12). When Christians give generously to meet the needs of others, gratitude flows to both God and others. When Paul thought of this marvelous economy of grace, he shouted, "Thanks be to God for his indescribable gift" (v. 15).

"His indescribable gift"

God's *gift* is what is freely given by Him. Paul described this gift as "indescribable." The use of the unique word *indescribable* is found only here in the New Testament. We do not even find it used in classical Greek. "Words fail Paul to describe the gift of Christ to and for us. He may have coined this word as it is not found elsewhere except in ecclesiastical writers save as a variant . . . 'wonder without description'" (A. T. Robertson, *Word Pictures in the New Testament*, "Epistles of Paul," vol. 4, 250).

The word *indescribable* means "not able to recount or to describe or to set forth in detail; God's exquisite working cannot be fully described with human words" (Fritz Rienecker, *Linguistic Key to the Greek New Testament* [Grand Rapids: Zondervan, 1980], 484).

Giving unifies all believers (vv. 13, 14). Through Christians who give generously from their hearts, God supplies the needs of all people. The reality of the matter is that true Christian giving affects "everyone else." In Paul's day, such giving served to unify Jewish and Gentile believers.

■ *In this section, Paul presented his theology of*
■ *giving. He offered guidelines for giving and*
■ *informed his readers that Christian giving is*
■ *based on the biblical understanding of God.*
■ *He went on to identify several results of the*
■ *ministry of giving: (1) giving supplies the*
■ *needs of God's people; (2) giving causes*
■ *God's people to overflow with thanksgiving*
■ *to God; and (3) giving serves to unify all*
■ *believers.*

QUESTIONS TO GUIDE YOUR STUDY

1. What guidelines did Paul offer for Christian giving?
2. Paul told his readers that Christian giving is based on the biblical understanding of God. What do we know about God that shapes our view of giving?
3. What results of Christian giving did Paul mention?
4. What is God's indescribable gift?

We see a noticeable change in the tone of Paul's letter as we move into chapters 10–13. Chapters 1–9 are characterized by comfort and confidence in both God and the Corinthians. From this point on in the letter, Paul engages in personal defense, replete with satire and sarcasm, and levels an attack against those who are negatively influencing the Corinthian believers. Clearly he is dealing with those who have opposed him or are determined to do so.

PAUL'S POTENTIAL FOR BOLDNESS (10:1–6)

Paul's words in these verses imply that he was being criticized as a coward. His critics claimed that he was bold when he wrote from afar, but humble when present before the Corinthians. Paul responded by appealing to the *meekness* and *gentleness* of Christ. That is the way Jesus chose to deal with people, and Paul would follow the example of his Lord. So he pleaded with the Corinthians not to force him to use strong tactics when he came, but rather he let them know that he was fully prepared to use his strength if necessary.

Paul went on to show that difference between his kind of strength and that of his critics. They were accusing him of living "by the standards of this world" (v. 2). Like the Gnostic heretics who came later, these critics prided themselves on being spiritual. Paul acknowledged that all live "in the world," the realm of human weakness, but he insisted that his ministry was being carried out on spiritual resources.

"Meekness" and "Gentleness"

Jesus described Himself as meek and declared that all with this character trait are blessed. Jesus exemplified meekness when He prayed that His enemies be forgiven (Luke 23:34). In translating Plato, Aristotle, and Plutarch, Matthew Arnold suggests "sweet reasonableness" for the Greek word translated in this verse as *gentleness*. A. T. Robertson says this kind of person "does not press for the last farthing of his rights."

"Stronghold"

This word is found only here in the New Testament. It is a military metaphor and refers to a stronghold or fortress. "It is used in a literal sense in Proverbs 21:22 (the Septuagint, the Greek translation of the Old Testament) while Philo uses it figuratively of a stronghold prepared by persuasive words against the honor of God (*Confusion of Tongues*, 129). But more important is the fact that the military practice of building strongholds (there was a large one on Acrocorinth) provided the imagery used in Cynic and Stoic philosophers, and in particular by Seneca, a contemporary of Paul, to describe the fortification of the soul by reasonable arguments to render it impregnable under attack of adverse fortune." (Colin Kruse, *Second Epistle of Paul to the Corinthians*, Tyndale New Testament Commentaries [Grand Rapids: Eerdmans, 1987], 174).

Paul knew he was fighting a spiritual war, but indicated that he had the necessary weapons to win. Although Paul did not specifically identify his weapon in this passage, he was confident that these weapons "have divine power to demolish strongholds" (v. 4). So equipped, Paul was ready to deal with the argument, pride, and rebellious thoughts of the enemy. He wanted all to understand that he would discipline those who had not been obedient to Christ.

- *Paul dealt with the charges of his critics, who*
- *claimed that he was showing timidity in*
- *face-to-face contacts, but operated with*
- *excessive boldness in the remote safety of a*
- *letter. In a meek and gentle approach, Paul*
- *insisted that his attitude and behavior were*
- *consistent, whether with the Corinthians or*
- *absent from them.*

PAUL ASSERTS HIS AUTHORITY (10:7–11)

Paul challenged the Corinthians to examine the facts, not what others were saying about him. The false teachers were claiming to belong to Christ in a unique way. There was even a "Christ party" in Corinth (1 Cor. 1:12). But if they were only to reflect on their experience with Paul, they would know that Paul belonged to Christ if anyone did. He had no fear that he would claim too much in his letters and then fail to live up to it in person. His letters may have seemed strong at times, but they were not simply an empty show of force. In effect, the false teachers were claiming, "Oh, his letters are fierce, but when you hear him in person he is unimpressive." Such accusations did not intimate Paul. He knew that his conduct in person matched his words, and that the Corinthians needed to understand this.

- In view of the charges from his critics, Paul
- challenged the Corinthians to examine the
- facts rather than listen to hearsay. The
- Corinthians' history with Paul was evidence
- that he belonged to Christ.

THE MEASURE OF A PERSON (10:12–18)

Paul did not intend to engage in comparing himself with the false apostles. They were comparing themselves with each other and their own standards. Paul knew that this was an unwise course for a servant of Christ. Taking his cue from the word *measure* (v. 12), Paul went on to speak of "limits" (vv. 13, 15). His critics questioned Paul's right to minister in Corinth. They wanted to declare the area "off limits" to him. Paul recognized that God had set limits to his ministry. His assignment was to go to the Gentiles and preach in new mission fields. Corinth was well within those guidelines. He had been the first to open the work in Corinth. He was certainly not overreaching himself to minister there. His goal was to enlarge the work in Corinth and then go on to other new fields. He would not, like the false apostles, work in someone else's field.

Lest he seem to be engaged in some sort of self-glorification contest with his critics, Paul reminded them that the only proper glorying for the believer is in God. After all, it is God's commendation, not one's own or any other person's, that matters.

"A wise man attacks the city of the mighty and pulls down the stronghold in which they trust" (Prov. 21:22).

Limits

This word is often translated "rule." It is also used to indicate *sphere of influence* and, in these cases, is translated "province, limits." (See William F. Arndt and F. Wilbur Gingrich, *A Greek-English Lexicon of the New Testament* [Chicago: U. of Chicago Press, 1957], 403.) According to Fritz Rienecker (*Linguistic Key to the Greek New Testament* [Grand Rapids: Zondervan, 1980], 487), it has to do with "rule, measuring rod, the fixed bounds of a territory. It may be that Paul has in mind the marked out lanes as used by runners in athletic contests."

- Paul's critics boasted of their ministry in
- Corinth and tried to claim credit for what
- Paul had accomplished there. Paul insisted
- that he would not boast of the work of
- another, but would boast only of what the
- Lord had done through him.

QUESTIONS TO GUIDE YOUR STUDY

1. Paul's approach to dealing with the Corinthians was one of meekness and gentleness. What do these terms mean? Why is it important for all Christians to take this same approach?
2. What is the "stronghold" that Paul referred to in verse 4?
3. How did Paul assert his authority with the Corinthians? What point did he drive home?
4. What did Paul consider to be the limits of his ministry?

2 CORINTHIANS 11

The Corinthian rebellion was serious enough to force Paul into the corner of self-defense. In this chapter, he turned his opponents' method of boasting on themselves.

THE THREAT OF "SUPER" APOSTLES (11:1–6)

Paul asked his readers to indulge him in some momentary foolishness for the sake of argument. In effect he was saying, "I'll play their little game." He did not want to boast or compare, but if that is what they wanted, he would show them he could do it better than they. He boasted of his jealousy over the Corinthian church, his generosity to the church, and his sufferings for the sake of the church. However, rather than engage in self-glory as his opponents did, he gave the glory to God.

Although he feigned foolishness, Paul was very serious. With deep feeling he told them that their relationship to Christ was a sacred marriage. This relationship was now being threatened by the false teachers who had undermined their devotion to Christ, just as the serpent seduced Eve in the Garden of Eden.

The false teachers spoke of Christ, but their presentation of Him was as though they were talking about a different Jesus. Their spirit and their gospel were different than Paul's, and he was disappointed that the Corinthian believers were so easily misled.

Paul boldly rejected the idea that he was inferior to the false teachers. He called them "super-apostles." They accused Paul of being unskilled; that is, a layman in speaking. The Greeks valued

"Deceived"

The word Paul used here (v. 3) means to be completely deceived, as was Eve. Paul feared that the Corinthians would buy the false apostles' teachings "hook, line, and sinker," and fall from their commitment to Christ.

False teachers preach a different gospel (11:4) based on human achievement. They demand payment for their services. They boast in their status and claim a superiority over their fellow Christians. They seek their own success and win influence over Christians by treachery and deceit. The church needs leaders who serve the church by proclaiming the lordship of Christ (4:5).

gifts of speech, and these teachers may have been well trained in oratory. But Paul knew, and the Corinthians had reason to know, that he was highly skilled in knowledge, even if a poor speaker by their standards. "I may not be a trained speaker, but I do have knowledge" (v. 6).

Support Ministry in the Early Church

In Old Testament life, the Temple tithe and offerings primarily supported the Levites and priests (Num. 18:20–24; Ezek. 44:28–30). Both Christ and Paul affirmed that supporting God-called ministers is the duty of the Christian church. Paul was anxious to assure the Corinthians that he was not after their money but desired that they know Christ. Paul apologized for permitting them to be "inferior" to other churches by not supporting his ministry. His self-support as a tentmaker was for their good and was not an example to be followed in all churches (from *Disciple's Study Bible* [Nashville: Broadman & Holman Publishers, 1988], 1484).

■ *Cunning, deceitful teachers were going to the*
■ *Corinthians and enticing Paul's friends away*
■ *from their pure commitment to Christ. Their*
■ *methods included attacking Paul's speaking*
■ *abilities and claiming a greater knowledge of*
■ *God's plans and workings than Paul. Paul*
■ *was concerned that the Corinthian believers*
■ *might accept the claims of the false apostles.*

PAUL REFUSES TO ACCEPT MONEY (11:7–11)

When Paul came to Corinth, he worked as a tent-maker with Aquila and Priscilla (Acts 18:1–3). It was customary for Jewish teachers to support themselves by a trade, but the Greeks considered manual labor beneath the dignity of a teacher.

The right of missionaries to be supported by the churches was clear to Paul, but he took special care at Corinth not to depend on the church financially (1 Cor. 9:6–15). He also accepted support from the churches of Macedonia rather than burden the Corinthians. His critics seem to have contended that these practices were not dignified enough for a true apostle, and perhaps they viewed this as a disgrace to the church. However, it was not from lack of love for the Corinthians that Paul refused their money. He dearly loved the believers there.

Paul had not accepted financial support from the Corinthians and insisted that he had never been a financial burden to them. His opponents wrongly interpreted this independence as evidence of Paul's lack of love for the Corinthians.

FALSE APOSTLES (11:12–15)

Paul's reason for consistently refusing financial support from the Corinthians was to show the contrast between himself and the false teachers. They claimed to be equal to Paul or even superior to him, yet they encouraged the Corinthians to support them financially. Paul realized that this put the false teachers at a disadvantage. His strongest attack on them came in verse 13. They were "false apostles, deceitful workmen, masquerading as apostles of Christ." Worse still, their behavior proved that they were servants of Satan, not apostles of Christ. Like Satan, they disguised themselves with the appearance of righteousness. Their future fate, Paul warned, would be appropriate. In 5:10, Paul reminded his readers that all must appear before the judgment seat some day. At that time, false teachers would face God's judgment.

"Angel of Light"

"The prince of darkness puts on the garb of light and sets the fashion for his followers in the masquerade to deceive the saints."

—A. T. Robertson

■ *Paul insisted that he would never change his*
■ *practice of refusing financial support*
■ *because his refusal to accept funds from the*
■ *Corinthians prevented his enemies from*
■ *boasting that they worked on the same basis.*

PAUL'S TACTICS AND THEIRS (11:16–21A)

This section begins Paul's celebrated "fool's speech." Paul did not want to be considered foolish; but since he was so accused, he intended to act the part to make his point. This boastful role had no divine authority in Paul's view. But as long as that was the game his opponents were playing, he would show that he could beat them by their own rules. There was, however, one important difference. They boasted of worldly things, whereas Paul boasted of his sufferings.

The Corinthians, Paul noted, had shown a willingness to be led by such aggressive, authoritarian tactics. He sarcastically called them "wise" because his approach had been termed "foolish." The false teachers had made slaves of the Corinthians, taken their money, and humiliated them (literally, "slap in the face"). If refusing to use such high-handed leadership was weakness, then Paul pleaded guilty to this weakness.

Paul's Boasts

BOAST	PASSAGE
His jealousy over the Corinthian church	vv. 1–6
His generosity to the Corinthians	vv. 7–21
His sufferings for the church at large	vv. 22, 23

THE CREDENTIALS OF A SERVANT OF CHRIST (11:21B–29)

Jewish Ancestry (vv. 21b, 22)

Paul then showed that he could match the "super-apostles" in a bragging match.

- They boasted of being Hebrews, those who spoke the language of their ancestors and read the sacred writings.
- They were Israelites, members of the chosen nation.
- They were heirs of Abraham and, therefore, to the promises made to him. But Paul was all of these, too.

Beyond Jewish Ancestry (vv. 23–27)

The false apostles passed the test of Jewish ancestry, but Paul asked, "Are they servants of Christ?" (v. 23). They called themselves servants of Christ. Paul not only matched them, he went far beyond them. The evidence he listed was not a string of victories; it was a list of hardships suffered. He, not they, showed the true marks of a servant of Christ: his sufferings. Most of the occasions listed do not appear in the book of Acts, which gives only a partial history of Paul's career.

Verses 23–37 list the many forms of persecution Paul had suffered, most of which came from his own people, the Jewish religious leaders.

Paul's Persecutions

STRENUOUS EXERTION:	• severe beatings • exposure to death • five times received thirty-nine lashes • three times beaten with rods
TRIALS OF TRAVEL:	• three times shipwrecked • robbers • dangerous rivers • dangers from false brothers
HARDSHIPS:	• sleeplessness • hunger • thirst • cold and nakedness

Verses 28, 29 tell of another kind of suffering, the pressures of a pastor-evangelist as he cared for his churches. Paul agonized daily with his converts as they encountered difficulties.

This, Paul wrote, is the kind of boasting an apostle should do. He must tell of his weakness, because that is where the strength of God touches the needs of people. Paul gave one more example, one that must have been well known to his friends (Acts 9:19–24). The picture of Paul being hidden in a basket and smuggled out of Damascus was not heroic. But it showed the courage and humility of the apostle and the providence of God in his life.

■ *Paul encountered opponents who boasted of*
■ *their apostolic credentials and questioned*
■ *Paul's. Paul had no option but to resort to the*
■ *foolish practice of boasting of his own cre-*
■ *dentials as an apostle in ministry.*

QUESTIONS TO GUIDE YOUR STUDY

1. What was the "foolishness" Paul took part in? Why did he ask the Corinthians to indulge him?

2. Paul refused to accept financial support from the Corinthian congregation. Why did he do this? Why did his decision not to take money create a problem for the false teachers?

3. What is a false teacher? What makes them dangerous to the church? How prevalent are false teachers in today's church?

4. What are the credentials of a true servant of Christ?

Criticism from Paul's opponents forced him to say what he did in this chapter. In the first part of the chapter, he shifted from his apostolic trials to issues of visions and revelation. In the second part, he assured the Corinthians that he had no interest in their money or material possessions. He gladly poured out his own possessions and personality for their benefit.

PAUL'S VISION (12:1–10)

Paul's opponents claimed that true apostles had special revelations. Therefore, the Corinthians may have thought that a spiritual leader should be able to point to visions and mystical experiences as qualification. It is probable that false prophets of Paul's day may have claimed such experiences themselves. In this passage, Paul let the Corinthians know that he experienced a vision, but he made it clear it was not the key to his effectiveness as a minister.

The "Third Heaven" (vv. 1–6)

Paul told his readers that he was caught up to the "third heaven" (v. 2). Jewish thought speculated that there were levels of heaven, as many as seven. The third level probably refers to the highest. So unusual was his experience that Paul twice remarked that he was not certain whether he was "in the body or apart from the body" (vv. 2, 3). The term *paradise* (v. 3), one Paul borrows from the Persians, means a park or garden.

In his account, Paul was reserved about the details of this experience and spoke as if it had happened to someone else. Paul's account did not relay what he saw—only what he heard. While caught up in paradise, Paul told his readers, he "heard inexpressible things, things that man is not permitted to tell" (v. 4). "The word was often used of divine secrets which were not intended for human beings" (Fritz Rienecker, *Linguistic Key to the Greek New Testament* [Grand Rapids: Zondervan, 1980], 494).

In speaking of himself, he spoke only of his "weaknesses," for it was in these that he found the real point of his ministry. His emphasis here makes it clear that he understood his mission was to preach the gospel of Christ, not visions.

Paul's Thorn in the Flesh (vv. 7–10)

It was possible that such an experience could have gone to Paul's head. But God was at work in Paul's life to prevent this from happening. God gave Paul a "thorn in my flesh" to ensure that he remained humble. Paul described this thorn as a "messenger of Satan" (v. 7). We do not know the exact nature of this thorn. Some have speculated that it may have been mental and spiritual anguish arising from the hardships he endured or his own grief over having persecuted the church. Most conclude that Paul is referring to a physical ailment of some sort. (For more information, see the article, "Paul's Thorn in the Flesh," at the back of this book.)

Whatever the thorn was, the lesson Paul learned from it is clear. Three times he asked God to remove the thorn, but God did not. It was God's design that Paul depend on His grace, not on Paul's own strength: "My grace is sufficient for you, for my power is made perfect in weakness" (v. 9). Because they were channels of God's power, Paul could affirm his disabilities.

■ *Paul related a time when he experienced the*
■ *inside of heaven. Although he disliked shar-*
■ *ing this account, he knew that God's strength*
■ *is more easily seen in the apostle's weakness.*
■ *In fact, God allowed Satan to afflict Paul to*
■ *keep him humble and to demonstrate the*
■ *power of God in his life. If his own vulnera-*
■ *bility revealed God's power, Paul gladly*
■ *accepted the weakness.*

FOOLISH TALK (12:11–13)

Having had to boast and draw so much attention to himself, Paul exclaimed, "I have made a
fool of myself" (v. 11). Rather than take this
approach to make his point, Paul should "have
been commended" by the Corinthians. He was
clearly grieved, for the believers at Corinth were
aware of Paul's ministry and sacrifices on their
behalf. His sacrifices and the changes in the lives
of the Corinthians were the "things that mark an
apostle" (v. 12). Paul mentioned three marks of
an apostle: signs, wonders, and miracles
("mighty works," NRSV).

Marks of an Apostle

MARK	MEANING	EMPHASIS
Signs	Miracles that convey a significance such as Jesus' seven signs in the Gospel of John	Appeal to one's understanding
Wonders	Unusual events that evoke awe on the part of those who witness them	Appeal to one's imagination
Miracles	Showed Paul's works to have a supernatural origin rather than a natural or human agent	Indicate a supernatural source

■ *Paul was grieved that he had to boast of him-*
■ *self to make the point of his genuine apostle-*
■ *ship. He added that the marks of an apostle*
■ *are signs, wonders, and miracles—all of*
■ *which were part of his divinely powered min-*
■ *istry to them.*

(For more information about signs, see the article "Signs" at the back of this book.)

PAUL REFUSES TO BE A BURDEN (12:14–18)

Paul had refused in the past to accept monetary support from the Corinthian church. Even though he had been criticized for doing so, he did not intend to change this position when he made his next visit. Paul's motivation for ministry was not gain but grace.

Ironically, his pure motive was interpreted as trickery by some in the congregation. Those helpers whom Paul had previously sent to Corinth to minister also did not take advantage of the people. Paul questioned the Corinthians to confirm that there was no evidence for this charge of trickery. "Did I exploit you through any of the men I sent you?" (v. 17). Clearly, Paul's policy in ministering to the believers in Corinth had been consistent.

■ *Paul planned to visit the Corinthians again.*
■ *As previously, he would again refuse their*
■ *money. Paul's ministry was characterized by*
■ *constant concern for people and a consis-*
■ *tency in both his actions and motives.*

A PASTOR'S CONCERN (12:19–21)

Paul now turned to the motives for his discussion in this chapter. The church at Corinth was an angry, divided church. A fear of Paul's was that his next arrival would find the believers there gripped by negative attitudes and actions. Here he attempted to build them up spiritually.

Paul listed eight kinds of sins, or vices, that he feared might exist at Corinth. His list here is similar to the one we find in his letter to the Galatians (5:19–21). The following chart shows these vices and provides a brief description for each.

Paul's List of Vices at Corinth

VICE	EXTENDED MEANING
Quarreling	Strife or rivalry among people
Jealousy	A mean spirit that begrudges the good of others
Outbursts of anger	A sudden flare-up of burning anger
Factions	Those who are selfish
Slander	Those who speak against others; backbiters
Gossip	Those who "whisper" behind the backs of others
Arrogance	Those who have an inflated opinion of themselves
Disorder	Out-of-control situations because people act without the thought of the common good

Paul closed this section of this letter by grieving over those who may have not repented of their former ways. He mentioned three sins that were formerly practiced by some of the Corinthian believers:

Impurity. This refers to uncleanness of any kind, and here, more specifically, to sexual sins of impurity.

Immorality. This refers to fornication or improper sexual relations.

Debauchery. This is a deliberate defiance of public decency. It is unrestrained and lawless insolence.

- *Fearing what he might find at Corinth, Paul*
- *alerted the Corinthian believers to several*
- *vices they must avoid. His goal was to*
- *strengthen the congregation and build them*
- *spiritually.*

QUESTIONS TO GUIDE YOUR STUDY

1. What kind of vision did Paul have? What was his purpose for relating it to the Corinthians?

2. What did Paul mean by a "thorn in my flesh" (v. 7)? Why did God allow Satan to so inflict Paul?

3. What are the marks of an apostle? What does each convey about Paul's ministry?

4. Why did Paul list the eight sins in verses. 19–21? What was he hoping to accomplish by discussing them?

This concluding chapter includes words of warning from Paul as he anticipated a visit to Corinth. The discipline of wrongdoers within the congregation was on his mind. Paul concluded his letter without the usual greetings, but he provided a unique trinitarian benediction.

"One witness is not enough to convict a man accused of any crime or offense he may have committed. A matter must be established by the testimony of two or three witnesses" (Deut. 19:15).

WORDS OF WARNING FROM PAUL (13:1–4)

Before his "third visit" (v. 1) to the Corinthians, Paul issued a stern warning. In this warning he cited Old Testament law to show that two or three witnesses served to establish charges. This implied that Paul intended to conduct a thorough investigation and discipline any wrongdoers in the Corinthian church.

To address any doubters, Paul spoke of his authority. He had been as weak as Christ was weak on the cross. But he could also show the strength of one who lives by the power of God.

■ *Paul claimed that he would not fail to make*
■ *another trip to visit the Corinthian believers.*
■ *He warned them that during this visit he*
■ *would deal with their sin firmly and in the*
■ *power of God.*

MEETING THE TEST (13:5–10)

Some had been judging Paul. To him, the real issue for them was not his authority but rather his opponents' own relationship with Jesus Christ. Rather than proving himself right, Paul was more concerned that his doubters succeed in their relationship to Christ. To them he issued two commands: "examine yourselves" and "test yourselves."

Examine yourselves (v. 5). The Corinthian believers needed to search their hearts to see that their attitudes were in keeping with the faith they professed.

Test yourselves (v. 5). This self-examination was to approve that they were indeed in Christ Jesus. "Such a testing of themselves will give them full knowledge that Paul is not reprobate. The best way for vacillating Christians to stop it is to draw close to Christ" (A. T. Robertson, *Word Pictures in the New Testament*, "Epistles of Paul," vol. 4, 270).

Meeting the Test

COMMAND	PURPOSE
"Examine yourselves"	To see whether one is "in the faith"
"Test yourselves"	To approve one's relationship with Christ after the examination

If Christ were not in these doubters, then they would have failed the only test that matters.

- Paul was concerned that his doubters suc-
- ceed in their relationship to Christ. In antic-
- ipation of his approaching visit, he issued
- two commands to them: "examine your-
- selves" and "test yourselves."

PAUL'S PARTING PLEA (13:11–13)

Paul's parting plea was a series of exhortations to his brothers and sisters in Christ at Corinth. In verse 11 he delivered the following exhortations.

"Aim for perfection." It is the same word he used in verse 9. The NRSV translates this phrase "put things in order." Mark, in his Gospel, used this word of James and John mending their nets. After the Corinthians made things right on the human level, they would enjoy fellowship with God on the divine level.

"Be of one mind." Paul encouraged the believers at Corinth to agree with one another, to think alike, and to be of the same mind.

"Live in peace." Each believer of the congregation was to be peaceable so each might live and work together in harmony. Those who did so would receive the promise that "the God of love and peace will be with you" (v. 11).

Holy Kiss

"In the Jewish synagogues where the sexes were separated, men kissed men, the women, women. This apparently was the Christian custom also. This custom is still observed in the Coptic and the Russian churches. It was dropped because of the charges made against the Christians by the pagans. In England in 1250 Archbishop Walter of York introduced a pax-board which was first kissed by the clergy and then passed around. Think of the germ theory of disease and that kissing tablet!"
—A. T. Robertson

Paul's Closing Exhortations

EXHORTATION	GOAL
Be restored to one another	Reconciliation
Be encouraged to agree with one another	Common purpose
Be at peace with one another	Harmony

- *Paul's parting plea was a series of exhortations*
- *to his brothers and sisters in Christ at Corinth.*
- *He exhorted them to be restored to one*
- *another, to be encouraged to agree with one*
- *another, and to be at peace with one another.*

PAUL'S THREEFOLD BLESSING FOR THE CORINTHIANS (13:14)

For a congregation desperately in need of God's love and fellowship of the Holy Spirit, Paul sent them a longer-than-normal final blessing. His last sentence has become a familiar benediction in public worship. "This benediction is the most complete of them all. It presents the persons of the Trinity in full form" (A. T. Robertson, *Word Pictures in the New Testament*, "Epistles of Paul," vol. 4, 271). "May the grace of the Lord Jesus Christ, and the love of God, and the fellowship of the Holy Spirit be with you all" (v. 14).

Paul's Trinitarian Benediction

PERSON OF THE TRINITY	BLESSING
Jesus Christ	Grace
God the Father	Love
Holy Spirit	Fellowship

■ *Paul concluded his letter with a beautiful*
■ *benediction. The benediction was trinitarian*
■ *in form and has played an important role in*
■ *the worship of God's people through the cen-*
■ *turies.*

QUESTIONS TO GUIDE YOUR STUDY

1. Why did Paul issue a stern warning to the Corinthians in verse 2?

2. In view of his approaching visit to meet with the Corinthians, Paul commanded them to "examine themselves" and "test themselves." What did Paul mean by these? What was his goal?

3. Paul left his readers with a series of closing exhortations. What were they and how applicable are they for today's congregations?
4. Describe Paul's benediction in verse 14. What makes it unique?

PAUL'S OPPONENTS IN CORINTHIANS

Paul faced severe attacks at Corinth. The Corinthian epistles reveal a general church disorder, a questioning of Paul's integrity, and an organized opposition from outside the church. In 1 Corinthians, however, the problems encountered arose from within the congregation. Groups within differed about how best to build the church, and they appealed to various leaders who had left their mark on the congregation (1 Cor. 1–3). Although this situation demanded a strong word, the proponents of this division did not attack Paul and the church as severely as outsiders did.

In 2 Corinthians, the opponents resembled those who opposed Paul elsewhere. Second Corinthians is the primary source for understanding the opponents at Corinth. The issues in 2 Corinthians involve Paul's character and calling.

The opponents used several avenues of approach in undermining Paul's authority. They said he had no credentials (2 Cor. 3:11). Paul responded by saying that the Corinthian Christians stood as his credentials. They said he had no confidence (2 Cor. 10). Paul responded with a theology of personal weakness that allowed the power of Christ to appear. They said he had no character (2 Cor. 1:17; 11:7). He responded by informing them that he followed the will of God for his life. Neither did he wish to burden them financially when he preached. They said he had no charisma (2 Cor 11:5, 6), to which he responded that he would not use the wisdom of the world to manipulate conversions. Finally, they claimed Paul had no calling (2 Cor. 3:12; 12:11). The apostle replied that his ministry was from God Himself (2 Cor. 5:20).

Additional attacks came from those concerned about Paul's seeming carelessness about the law. Some have interpreted Paul's opponents to have been Gnostic. The immediate issues, however, focused on the place of the law in the believer's life. These include the relationship of law and grace (2 Cor. 3:1–8).

Furthermore, Paul defended himself against an attack on his true Jewishness by a comparison to other Jewish apostles (2 Cor. 11:22). The concern for the law was mixed with a concern for some of the finer points of oratory that were practiced so well at Corinth.

Paul defended himself because the purity of the gospel was at stake. He would not allow anyone to capture his converts and bring them under a legal code. The gospel would not be trivialized by using rhetorical devices of manipulation. At Corinth, therefore, Paul's opposition came from both Jewish and Gentile sources. The primary opposition, however, came from Jews with some exposure to Christianity intent on reaffirming the law as a vital part of Christian faith.

(From the *Holman Bible Handbook*, pp. 706–07.)

SIGNS

A sign is something which points to something else; an object, occurrence, or person through which one recognizes, remembers, or validates something; military signal (Josh. 2:12); military standard (Num. 2:2; Ps. 74:4). Signs may be classed according to seven somewhat overlapping functions:

1. *Signs can impart knowledge or give identity*. These signs typically characterize God as Lord of history and champion of oppressed Israel (e.g., Exod. 7:5; 8:22; 10:2).

2. *Signs protect*. The mark of Cain (Gen. 4:15), blood on the doorposts at Passover (Exod. 12:13), and the seal of God upon the foreheads protected those under the sign (Rev. 9:4).

3. *Signs motivated faith and worship*. Israel's unbelief in spite of signs is often condemned (Num. 14:11, 22; Deut. 1:29–33). The signs fulfill

their goal when they inspire obedience (Deut. 11:3, 8), worship (Deut 26:8, 10), and loyalty to the Lord (Josh. 24:16, 17).

4. *Signs serve as reminders of significant events.* Eating unleavened bread at Passover (Exod. 13:9) and redeeming the firstborn (Exod. 13:16) are reminders of God's liberation of Israel.

5. *Other signs serve as reminders of a covenant or established relationship.* Rainbow, covenant with Noah (Gen. 9:12–17); circumcision, covenant with Abraham (Gen. 17:11; Rom. 4:11); Sabbath, covenant with Moses (Exod. 31:13, 17; Ezek. 20:12). The Lord's Supper points to Jesus' new covenant.

6. *Signs serve as confirmation.* Signs often authenticated God's special call of Moses (Exod. 3:12; 48); of Gideon (Judg. 6:17); of Saul (1 Sam. 10:2–9), and confirmed God's word of judgment (1 Sam. 2:34; Jer. 44:29–30) or promise of healing (2 Kings 20:8).

7. *Signs take the form of prophetic acts.* The names of Isaiah ("Yahweh is salvation") and his sons Shear-jashub ("A remnant shall return") and Maher-shalal-hash-baz ("The spoil speeds, the prey hastens") illustrate Israel's fate (Isa. 7:3; 8:3).

The New Testament often rebukes the demand for a sign to confirm God's work (Matt. 16:1; John 2:18; 5:48; 1 Cor. 1:22). A sign may evoke faith in a receptive heart, but no sign will convince the hard-hearted.

(From the *Holman Concise Bible Dictionary*, p. 605.)

PAUL'S THORN IN THE FLESH

In 2 Corinthians 12:7, Paul referred to a "thorn in the flesh," "a messenger of Satan, given him by God to ensure his humility. The nature of this "thorn in the flesh" has been the subject of many speculations. Guesses ranging from epilepsy (a popular conjecture of classical liberalism, which sought to offer rational explanations for Paul's visionary experiences, especially his conversion), malaria (because of its prevalence in some of the regions of Paul's ministry), and eye disease (because of the unusual metaphorical expression in Gal. 4:15) have been suggested.

A more acceptable solution, however, relates to the context of 2 Corinthians 12:1–10 where "thorn in the flesh" parallels both "messenger of Satan" in verse 7 and the "weaknesses," "insults," "distresses," "persecutions," and "difficulties" of verse 10. The Old Testament use of the term *thorn* also offers some help. In Num. 33:55 and Ezek. 28:24 we read of enemies who are "thorns" in Israel's side, a constant harassment to Israel as the agent of the Lord's redemptive judgments (cp. Josh. 23:13; Hos. 2:6).

Therefore, in 2 Cor. 12:7, "thorn in the flesh" refers more to the enemy, the "messenger of Satan," than to any specific physical ailment. The "messenger of Satan" was a redemptive judgment (as Israel's enemies were also used) of God upon Paul "to keep me from exalting myself." Thus, Paul's entire apostolic experience of suffering (cp. 2 Cor. 1:3–11; 4:7–5:10; 6:1–10; 7:2–7; 11:16–33), abetted by Satan and operative through the evils of this world, was the "messenger of Satan," a "thorn in the flesh," which God gave and used to keep the great apostle humbly obedient. Paul could truly say that he was an earthen vessel (4:7), one who shared the sufferings of Christ (1:5), so that the life of Jesus might be manifested through his very mortality (4:11); "for when I am weak, then I am strong" (12:10).

(From the *Holman Bible Dictionary*, p. 1344.)

The following list is a collection of the source works used for this volume. All are from Broadman & Holman's list of published reference resources. These sources can accommodate the reader's need for more specific information and for an expanded treatment of the material in 2 Corinthians. All of these works will greatly aid in the reader's study, teaching, and presentation of Paul's second letter to the Corinthians. The accompanying annotations can be helpful in guiding the reader to the proper resources.

Adams, J. McKee, rev. by Joseph A. Callaway, *Biblical Backgrounds*. This work provides valuable information on the physical and geographical settings of the New Testament. Its many color maps and other features add depth and understanding.

Blair, Joe, *Introducing the New Testament*, pp. 140–42. Designed as a core textbook for New Testament survey courses, this volume helps the reader in understanding the content and principles of the New Testament. Its features include special maps and photos, outlines, and discussion questions.

Cate, Robert L., *A History of the New Testament and Its Times*. An excellent and thorough survey of the birth and growth of the Christian faith in the first-century world.

George, David C., *2 Corinthians, Galatians, Ephesians*, Layman's Bible Book Commentary, vol. 21 (Nashville: Broadman & Holman Publishers, 1980), pp. 13–49. A popular-level treatment of 2 Corinthians. This easy-to-use volume provides a relevant and practical perspective for the reader.

Holman Bible Dictionary. An exhaustive, alphabetically arranged resource of Bible-related subjects. An excellent tool of definitions and other information on the people, places, things, and events of the Bible.

Holman Bible Handbook, pp. 696–700. A comprehensive treatment that offers outlines, commentary on key themes and sections, and full-color photos, illustrations, charts, and maps. Provides an accent on the broader theological teachings.

Holman Book of Biblical Charts, Maps, and Reconstructions. A colorful, visual collection of charts, maps, and reconstructions, These well-designed tools are invaluable to the study of the Bible.

Lea, Thomas D., *The New Testament: Its Background and Message*, pp. 425–36. An excellent resource for background material—political, cultural, historical, and religious. Provides background information in broad strokes on specific books, including the Gospels.

McQuay, Earl P., *Keys to Interpreting the Bible.* This work provides a fine introduction to the study of the Bible that is invaluable for home Bible studies, lay members of a local church, or students.

McQuay, Earl P., *Learning to Study the Bible.* This study guide presents a helpful procedure that employs the principles basic to effective and thorough Bible study. Using Philippians as a model, the various methods of Bible study are applied. Excellent for home Bible studies, lay members of a local church, and students.

Robertson, A. T., *A Grammar of the Greek New Testament in the Light of Historical Research.* An exhaustive, scholarly work on the underlying language of the New Testament. Provides advanced insights into the grammatical, syntactical, and lexical aspects of the New Testament.

Robertson, A. T., *Word Pictures in the New Testament*, "Epistles of Paul," vol. 4, pp. 205–71. This six-volume series provides insights into the language of the New Testament—Greek. Provides word studies as well as grammatical and background insights into the epistles of Paul.